Just To Make You Smile
A teenage daugher's reflections on loving and losing her father to ALS

Sarah Caldwell

Dedication

For Sharon and Kathryn
Keep on Trekking

Acknowledgements

Everyone named in this book has a special place in my heart; you have touched me in ways you will never know possible. But to all the people behind the scenes, you have touched me just as much, because all I have done has been a direct result of the help and support I have received from you.

To those of you who showed up at that very first Walk to Defeat ALS in September 2013, you gave me the courage to move forward to help fight this disease. To those of you who wore red at school the week after my dad died and then again the following year, thank you for showing me how much love there is in the world. To those of you who still wear a Red Trekkers bracelet to this day — yes I see you, and yes I want to cry every time I see that flash of red, because it means that much to me.

To my beloved teachers at Falmouth High School: Amy Magnuson, Lynn Harder, Joanna Leary, Lee Fortier, Sue Leonard, and many more. Thanks for being more than teachers to me, for keeping me in check all these months later. But also for teaching me everything I know — because that's pretty important too. A special shout out to Amy

Magnuson for all the life lessons and emails at 5 a.m. and for being the first person to read this book. To Holly MacEwan, for helping me start this whole thing in the first place. Thank you to high school principal Gregg Palmer for always having my back in what I have done for my ALS campaign.

To my gymnastics coaches, Jamian and JJ, and my teammates, Anna, Emma, Serina, and all the other little minions — thanks for always picking me back up when I fall. Thank you to all my friends at school who supported me during some very dark times and were there to stay up into the wee hours of the morning to cry — you have no idea how much you saved me.

Thank you to all the people at the ALS Association, particularly Amy Coyne and Nell Davies. Thank you to Dr. Nazem Atassi for looking over the sections on ALS in this book and to Dr. Merit Cudkowicz for answering all my crazy questions. Thank you to anyone who has ever interviewed me for all the work I have done and helped me share my story.

To Prudential and John Strangfeld, I am forever grateful, because without you and the opportunity you gave me as a Prudential Spirit of Community honoree, I would never have written a book.

To my wonderful editor and publisher, Allison, who took on the unthinkable task of signing a contract with a seventeen-year-old girl with no previous writing experience — you're a brave soul, I hope I was worth it!

To Steve Gleason, for writing the foreword, and to all other people living with ALS — you are the ultimate inspiration in my life. Together, we will find a cure. To Karen, for being that person who "gets me," inspiring me to write this book in the first place. To Rachel, for coming up with the title — I am forever in debt to you. To my Aunt

Barbara and Uncle Bruce for being second parents to me. To my sister Kathryn, for becoming a best friend to me. Dad always did say it would happen.

To my mother, Sharon Leskanic. You are the shining light in my life. I won't even try to thank you for all you've done.

And finally, of course, thank you to my father, Jim Caldwell. For teaching me the important things in life. I love you. I hope your golf swing is that much better in heaven.

Foreword

When asked to write this foreword, I was honored, but I also knew it would be a challenge. Like Sarah's father, I have ALS. Her book is written from the perspective of a young girl who is witnessing her father's disease progression and ultimately, his passing. Somehow, through it all, Sarah found the strength to capture her thoughts in this book as an effort to inspire other young people who may have a sick parent.

As a parent living with ALS, I am inspired, seeing how Sarah found strength as her father's waned. One thing I've learned while living with ALS is this disease is not short on heroes. From all those fighting to survive, to their caregivers, to the family members, friends and supporters, ALS takes ordinary people and catapults them to hero status. Sarah is one of those heroes. She not only survived a tragic situation with dignity, she is offering to share what she learned, with the intention of helping others who may be struggling in a similar situation.

The fight to end ALS needs people like Sarah. She has committed herself to working toward an end to the disease. If her commitment to eradicate ALS is anything like her commitment to her father, we are in good hands.

Thank you Sarah…. keep smiling.

~Steve Gleason, former New Orleans Saints NFL safety
Diagnosed with ALS in 2011

"If you are going through hell, keep going."
~ Winston Churchill

"Our greatest glory is not in never failing, but in rising up every time we fail."
~ Ralph Waldo Emerson

Introduction

My name is Sarah Caldwell. I am seventeen years old. My dad was diagnosed with the disease ALS — also known as Lou Gehrig's disease — when I was fifteen years old; he passed away just sixteen months later. ALS is a neurological disease that gradually robs a person of his or her ability to walk, talk, and eventually breathe. The whole time, the mind is typically alert and functional. At fifteen, I found out my dad was going to die through finding a bottle of his medication. At sixteen, I found out he had died when my mom came to get me at gymnastics practice and, through tears, told me Dad hadn't made it.

Doctors on TV (and I'm sure in real life too, but I'm not a doctor) are taught to spell out the situation when someone passes and literally say, "He died." Saying, "He didn't make it," or, "We did everything we could," simply doesn't cut it. I didn't understand that until my mom told me, "Dad didn't make it." I didn't understand what she was saying. I had seen my dad that morning, and he was still talking and walking and smiling. There's no way he could be gone…could he? But in fact, I had been left without my father, my mentor, my hero. This man would not be there to tear up when I graduated from high school or walk me down the aisle when I got married. At age sixteen, I was put in a situation few people my age have experienced. And I didn't even get to say goodbye.

This memoir is the story of my journey through my dad's diagnosis, death, and what I have chosen to do to carry on his legacy. After my dad was diagnosed with ALS, I felt as though I didn't have anyone to turn to who was experiencing a similar situation. I didn't know anyone else my age who had a dying parent, and when I looked for books, I couldn't find any that could help me. I didn't know if what I was feeling was normal. Was I supposed to have feelings of resentment toward my dad for being sick? To lie on the floor and cry myself to sleep every night? It was months of depression, anger, and denial before I finally woke up and literally picked myself up off the ground. I chose to do everything I could to live without any regrets in the time I had left with him and stand beside my hero in his battle with ALS.

I helped him go swimming with stingrays and swing a golf club again. I encouraged him that he wasn't missing much by not being able to eat dinner with us anymore ("Sorry Mom, the chicken is dry"), and I made riding in a wheelchair fun (picture me racing him across the room and "accidentally" flipping him over). More importantly, I helped do something about his greatest frustration: there is no cure or effective treatment for ALS. I helped found a group, Team Red Trekkers, to raise awareness of ALS and fundraise to help find a cure. Less than a month later, my dad lost his battle with this disease. ALS had defeated him. But then again, it hadn't. My dad had maintained his positive attitude up until the end, and he never blamed anyone for his disease. I honestly don't know if I would ever be able to do that; I would probably blame my parents for "giving me bad genes" as I do whenever I get sick. Even after my dad died, I wasn't about to stop fighting ALS. I wanted to carry on my dad's mission to find a cure. My campaigns have touched people nationwide, raising awareness of and funding for this currently incurable disease.

After my dad died, I was introduced to a girl my age, Karen, whose mom was diagnosed with ALS. As I wrote this book, I started giving her drafts as I made progress, and, every time, I could see the weight of sorrow lift off her shoulders just a little. She no longer was alone. If this book has the potential to reach just one person like Karen, just one person who realizes what they are feeling is normal, then I can know my contribution to the world has truly made a difference. I will have helped someone who needs help, the exact thing that I needed all those months ago when my family's journey with ALS first began.

Chapter One

The very first memory I have of my childhood is walking along a beach in Sanibel Island, Florida with my mom and dad. I keep stopping to pick up shells, the coarse sand harsh against my small toes. I can't fit them all in my hand and I begin to drop them. A woman walks up to us and gives me a plastic snack bag to put my shells in. I look at the bag and think that it is a different type of snack bag than the ones that my mom buys; there is no "zipper" as I call it. I look up at the woman and smile and murmur a "thank you," something that my mom and dad always told me to say, because it is polite.

And that's it. I have no more memories of anything until my sister Kathryn was born six months later. Why I chose to hang on to this memory, I have no idea; something in my mind told me it was important. I think about this story often and wonder how much of it is really true. I mean, I was two years old, how much of it could possibly be true? How much of it could I have possibly absorbed and remembered? Even so, I still see the same face of the woman every time; she has wispy brown hair, a gentle smile, and is wearing a white sundress. I've always wondered if someone was with her or if she was just walking alone. A few nights ago I finally asked my mom about this woman, but she doesn't remember her. Did she really exist? I want to go ask my dad too, but I can't. He died exactly one year ago. It's instances like this, instances where I want to ask my dad something so badly, but just can't, that will always trigger that wave of sadness that I know oh so well.

Childhood is a gift—always remember that. I guess a seventeen-year-old really shouldn't be preaching about childhood—I am still a child, after all, and my mom still does my laundry and makes me dinner — but in many ways I'm not as much of a child as I probably should be. I've had to learn how to advocate for myself, how to carry on difficult conversations, and how to live in this world without my father, all things that aren't supposed to happen until later in life. If I had known this was going to be my journey, my fate, would I have taken it? Well, I guess I wouldn't have much of a choice. I have to grow up sometime, after all. But would I have done anything differently? Absolutely.

I was a bratty kid. There, I admit it. Even to this day, I tend to live in my own little world sometimes, spending more time doing homework or at gymnastics practice — surviving daily life, as I call it — than with my family. I am incredibly pleasant and likable at school and everywhere else, but at home, I tend to let loose. After all, I have to take all my anger out somewhere, right?

This little pattern seems like the norm for kids these days, particularly hormone-raged teenagers who think the sun revolves around their social schedules. After all, your family will always love you no matter what, right? You can shoot them down and be rude all you want, but in the end, the love is always unconditional, right? In school, if you are mean to friends, they will abandon you and talk behind your back. If you are inconsiderate to teachers, you will get suspended. If you are rude to a coach, you will get kicked out of practice. But at home, for the most part, it's much harder to get thrown out.

As my mom will say, even back to when I was two years old, I used to throw huge fits over the dumbest things, from not getting the instrument I wanted in music class to not getting the toy I wanted at my birthday. Notice a pattern here? It is all about material items. I wouldn't be surprised if I got mad over the fact that I didn't find a shell that I wanted on the beach that day. I eventually learned it was socially unacceptable to throw fits in public, so I gradually restrained my meltdowns to home. After all, as long as my friends and teachers liked me, what did it matter if my family did?

So that was the gist of my life at home, particularly when it came to my dad. In fourth grade when I didn't understand my math homework and asked him for help, I would get frustrated and yell at him because he simply did not understand the directions. My dad was a smart man. He was valedictorian of his high school, graduated from Cornell University with a degree in engineering, held significant positions in the semiconductor industry for almost thirty years, and then ran his own business to help companies reduce costs. But somehow, I still didn't think he was smart enough, that he was worthy enough to spend my Friday nights with, that his opinion mattered.

Then in eighth grade, whenever my dad drove me anywhere, I was more apt to be on my phone texting friends than talking to him. I was more likely to think some Facebook status or a text about the latest relationship drama at school was more important than whatever my dad, the person physically sitting right next to me and giving up his time to be my shuttle bus home, had to say. He got incredibly frustrated that I would not talk to him, and I always responded with a sassy, "What do you want me to talk about?"

It is only when I began driving my sister around years later, her doing the same exact thing, that I finally found an answer to that question I would ask my dad every time we were together: anything. He wanted to talk about anything. The silence of the car as someone sits beside you, disinterested in you, is almost as painful as someone saying he or she does not like you. Silence is the ultimate stab in the heart, the ultimate declaration of, "I do not care what you have to say." I certainly can admit that at times, this is what I was thinking; I did not care what my dad said because I thought it would be dumb or boring or pointless. After all, I was obviously smarter than him.

Like most teenagers, I thought my dad was the biggest embarrassment of my life. At parent-teacher conferences he would ask question after question, from the minor details to the random things he came up with, all of which didn't hold a whole lot of substance, "just for clarification." Then he would bring out his miniature notebook and jot some notes down in his scrawly little handwriting and say, "What was that? Can you repeat that, please?" for about the fourteenth time. I cannot tell you how many times I blew up after one of these things and told him he "embarrassed me" with his questions, to which he would reply, "Sarah, be pleasant. I'm just trying to understand what you're doing in school."

I always thought my dad was awkward when interacting with my friends, and I felt as though I was permanently stuck in two-year-old world when he would talk in third person. It was always, "Mom and Dad have something to talk about," and, "Time for night nights. It's already ten o'clock." Our conversations were dominated by his typical phrase of, "I missed that," and my typical sassy response of, "Dad, it doesn't matter," which was subsequently followed by an argument that involved me yelling and him just rationally standing there watching me flip out, ending the conversation with, "Sarah, just be nice," and walking away.

My dad wasn't one to complain or fight. I know dads who can literally become scary when they get mad, turning bright red and screaming at the top of their lungs. My dad seldom got worked up, but when he did — usually as the result of something I said — it was, as I have come to realize, for just reasons. Still, at the time, I would run up to my bedroom, screaming and crying and all bloodshot in the eyes, screaming, "Why are you so mean to me?" and, "Life is not fair!" I would feel sorry for myself, and expect someone to come to my room to comfort me. But no one ever did. Because the things I was crying about were trivial, unimportant, childish.

I would cry about the consequences of my actions and blame it on others. But this crying was superficial; there were no deeper feelings other than, "why are my parents so mean?" and, "life is not fair." No, my parents were not mean; they were the most loving parents I could ever have asked for. I, in fact, was the one who was being mean. And no, life is not fair. But my perfect little life, the bubble I was living in, was certainly a step up from what most people experience. At the time, I had no idea what it truly meant for life to be unfair, for there to appear to be nothing but flaws in the fate you envision yourself having.

Everyone has a fate in life. Your life is altered in small ways every single day, from the development of plaque in your arteries when you choose bacon over cereal to the friend you make when you are coincidentally seated next to a person on an airplane who chooses to smile at your first interaction rather than swiftly avoid eye contact.

Then there are those bigger moments, like when you find out you are going to have a baby sister, when you discover your love for a sport, when you first become a "big kid" and enter middle school, and when you get your first dog. There may be a fight with a friend here and there, a bad grade on a test, or an unsuccessful audition. These are all blips on the radar, and life will inevitably go on no matter how bad it seems in the moment.

But then there are those moments that completely alter the course of your life. Those events are so big they almost seem unreal. They are irreversible and make you realize nothing will ever be the same again. Many people may never have a moment in their life like this until they grow up and go out into the "real world." But I did.

* * * * *

May, 2012

My dad had been acting strange. He had had a persistent cough for the past few months that just wouldn't seem to go away. Every time I would ask him about it, he always said it was "nothing" and "no big deal," because he got a cough every year and it would just go away. He said he was fine. But even after hearing the same response over and over again, something told me this was a bit different. This cough wasn't going away.

Then one night while I was in the car with him, he started coughing and couldn't seem to catch his breath. He was gasping for air with every breath, all the while continuing the conversation we were having. All of a sudden I became very angry. He was sick. He was not fine.

I started yelling at him. I told him he needed to go to the doctor and putting it off any longer was not an option. For all the crap I gave my dad, I had never ordered him to do anything. Until then. Tears welled in my eyes. I knew something was wrong. The car went silent. He didn't say anything for several seconds. He had a look on his face I couldn't decipher. Then finally, he opened his mouth. "Okay, I will," were his only words. Then he went silent again.

Just like that, he gave in. I don't know if he already had an appointment scheduled or if this was the last straw, but he did end up going to the doctor a week later. Although I knew something was wrong, I had reassured myself that the doctor would tell him it was just a cold. I had reassured myself that he truly was okay. And with that, I forgot about the appointment. I had forgotten because I brushed off any feelings of worry, because I thought everything was going to be okay. As it turns out, it wasn't. I had no idea that doctor's appointment was the beginning of an unthinkable journey, a journey whose path we had already glimpsed.

* * * * *

My mom was diagnosed with a rare form of sarcoma cancer in July, 2010. She immediately had surgery to remove a football-sized tumor from her abdomen. The prognosis was not good, especially given the size of the mass and a quick reoccurrence two months later. However, throughout everything, my parents were very forthright with my sister Kathryn and me. They told us straight up that this was a bad cancer and that the doctors didn't know if she would make it.

I think it was only natural for us to go into defense mode and pretend like it wasn't happening. We couldn't imagine life without a mother. Even after several grueling months of radiation and a second surgery, the doctors didn't know what to expect. But today, four years later, she is in remission. She truly should not be here right now, but somehow, she beat the odds.

Throughout this whole journey, my parents always made sure to keep Kathryn and me in the loop on everything. I knew when she was going in for initial tests, when she was going in for surgery, when they found out it was cancer, and when they found out it had reoccurred.

They never kept secrets, and if I asked, they would tell. They told us right away as soon as they knew anything.

So it was a bit of a surprise to me when I found out my dad had, in fact, gone to the doctor and neither he nor my mom told us anything. When I tried to ask questions about the appointment and about what had happened, all my mom and dad would say was that he was going to see another doctor. They would not say why. A few weeks later, my mom told me he was having tests done at the hospital, including many CAT scans and MRIs. I didn't understand why. He had a cough, but other than that, I thought, he was fine.

* * * * *

June 15th, 2012

On the last day of school my dad had a doctor's appointment. We were leaving that afternoon to go to Texas to visit friends, so Mom's best friend Lisa picked Kathryn and me up from school and we met my parents in the Subway parking lot by the airport. We stepped out of the car and I immediately knew something was wrong. My mom was overly smiley and my dad just seemed pretty quiet. They didn't say anything about the appointment. It was just something about they way they looked that caused me to begin to doubt all the "Dad is fine" speeches I had tried to give myself. I knew something was wrong.

I asked if I could go to Subway and get something to eat. I'm allergic to gluten (i.e. bagels, pasta, cookies, and anything with that flaky and delicious look), so I couldn't get a sandwich, and I was tired of eating salads. All I wanted was a few slices of turkey breast. But apparently they couldn't just give me turkey because that was not an option on the cash register. Kathryn was getting a sandwich so they gave me two slices of turkey and called it "extra meat" and then shooed us away as the next customer came up in line. I was furious. I was hungry and there wasn't anything else in the area I could eat. I thought of complaining and making a big deal about it, but then I realized we had to go so we weren't late to the airport. At the time my too-small stack of turkey seemed like my biggest problem in life, and I was left to contemplate my unfortunate situation all the way to the airport. I decided I wasn't ever going to that Subway again.

When we got in the car, I asked how the appointment went. "Fine," was all my mom said. Nothing else. As we drove to the airport, a feeling of uneasiness was heavy in the air. My parents were talking about things like how warm it was going to be in Texas and how exciting that it was finally Summer Vacation, things to fill the space, to prevent the air from being void of conversation, to ensure my parents' secret would not fall heavy on their shoulders in the moment of silence.

The trip down was fairly uneventful, other than my dad's frequent coughing. It had become a given when we were around him: plan for Jim to interrupt every few words he is saying with a cough. But he still seemed normal—he was still the one who took charge through the airport, taking his wallet out to tip the luggage carrier and getting the rental car to drive us to my aunt and uncle's house.

The next morning we drove to Austin to see my parents' friends, Jan and Jean-Claude. It was JC's sixtieth birthday and they were hosting a party at their house that night. When we got there, Kathryn and I helped prepare the food and my mom and Jan caught up on life. My dad went upstairs to take a nap. Jan would later tell me she knew something was wrong from the moment he walked through the door. She thought it was his arthritis acting up or something.

I guess when you are always around someone you just don't notice the subtle changes. I didn't notice yet how his gait was different, his speech slower and slightly slurred. I didn't notice how he was moving slowly overall. All I noticed was the cough; the cough was all I *wanted* to notice, and any other changes I pushed aside and blamed them, as Jan did, on his arthritis or his "old age."

That night my parents strategically placed themselves slightly away from the hype of the growing party, sitting by the pool, talking over a glass of wine. I watched them from a distance. They seemed to be in an intense conversation. I started walking towards them and the conversation slowed, but my mom kept that look on her face, that look I could not figure out.

"Do you want to go to Paris with Dad?" my mom asked. Just like that. No hello or asking me if I am having fun— she was straight up giving me a trip to Paris with my dad.

I should have been ecstatic and jumping up in down. But I wasn't. For the first time I saw right into my dad's eyes. I saw pain. For the first time, I saw him vulnerable. He still hadn't said anything. If I hadn't already noticed things were a bit strange, my father taking me on the trip of a lifetime, seemingly for no reason, would have been enough of an indication that something was wrong. I knew whatever was going on was more than just a cough. It was something much, much more.

* * * * *

July 11th, 2012

On a seemingly normal Wednesday night just a few weeks later, my mom went to visit Kathryn at basketball camp and I was left home alone with my dad. I needed to find a book for a summer English assignment, and my mom had said she read the one I wanted and it was somewhere in her room. She hadn't had time to look for it, and I was getting impatient because I knew I needed to start soon. So that night I dug through her bookshelf and her nightstand to no avail. Then, for some reason, I opened the drawer in the cabinet next to my dad's side of the bed. There was an old baby monitor, some tissues, a notebook, and a bottle of medication, but no book.

I took a second glance at that medication. It seemed a bit weird that there was medication in his nightstand. He'd always kept all his medication for his arthritis in the bathroom, and I knew what it looked like because ever since I was little he would always show me it and warn me to never touch it because "bad things could happen" if I accidentally ate it. But this little orange bottle was different. It was smaller and the pills were shaped differently.

I looked on the label. It said *Rilutek,* and it was prescribed by a doctor that I had not heard him mention before. I went back to my room — without the book I had been searching for in the first place — and typed *Rilutek* into Google.

I clicked on the first site that came up. I was brought to a page that had a blue banner across the top and a picture of a man and woman, both with white hair, sitting on a beach and smiling. The website looked like the typical drug company website, with the people smiling because all their problems were solved because of this drug.

I scrolled through the website and came across the term 'ALS.' I knew I had heard about ALS before but I had no idea what it is. I remembered a recent article in *People* magazine about Buddy Valastro of TLC's *Cake Boss* and how his mother had been recently diagnosed with ALS. The cover said something about how they were going to "fight ALS together with Momma." I knew what MS — muscular sclerosis — was because I had done a project on it for school, and for some reason I remember thinking of ALS as similar to that. I knew MS made a person's limbs a bit weak, but was not fatal. I hadn't had time to read the article in *People* and I hadn't bothered to look up ALS.

I typed ALS into Google. It's just three small letters, three powerless letters. There's no way it could be bad, right? I clicked on the first link, leading me to the PubMed webpage. It seemed very official. There was a whole list of symptoms, including difficulty walking, decreased finger dexterity, problems breathing, and changes in speech, but nothing about a cough.

Scrolling down, I came to the prognosis section. Two lines stood out to me above all. *Death often occurs within three to five years. There is no known cure.*

People talk about a pit in their stomach when they are nervous, but I didn't know it could actually happen. In that instant, it did. In that instant, my life changed forever. The world became fuzzy and I felt like I was going to pass out. My head felt heavy, my heart like it was about to explode. Then the tears came, and boy did they come. My dad was going to die. My sweet, loving, caring, and wonderful-in-every-way dad was going to leave me before he could watch Kathryn and me grow up.

What happened next I cannot exactly remember. I know I sobbed for a long time — so long I blew some blood vessels in my face and eyes. For the first time in my life, I was actually crying about something that was more than me feeling sorry for myself. Even with Mom's cancer, I cannot recall a time in which I actually cried. Up until that point, most of my tears shed had been for the trivial inconveniences, the things that made me say, "life is not fair." But this time, I was crying for something worth crying about. It was also the first time no one else knew I was crying, the first time I wasn't waiting for someone to open the door. I was crying because, at this moment, life was truly unfair.

My dad was going to die. And I had no one to tell, no one to talk to about it. If my mom and dad had wanted me to know, they would have told me, right? But they hadn't. Suddenly I was overcome with anger as questions flooded through my overwhelmed brain. Why would they have withheld this information from me? How could this have been Dad's diagnosis if all he had was a cough? But then the most overwhelming, the scariest, and the most important question flowed through my brain: how long would he have to live?

I would only find out that answer after he had succumbed to the effects of this insidious disease. And this answer, to much dismay and shock, would turn out to be less than two years.

Chapter Two

Before I go any further, I suppose a description of ALS is necessary. Many people have heard of it but most do not know what it really is. So here is my best attempt at an explanation.

Amyotrophic lateral sclerosis (ALS), commonly referred to as Lou Gehrig's Disease, is a progressive and fatal degenerative neurological disease that causes motor neurons to die. ALS usually affects people between ages forty and sixty, but it can strike people of all ages. Motor neurons are the nerves that control most of our voluntary movements. Motor neurons are of two types: upper motor neurons which branch from the brain and connect with the spinal cord, and lower motor neurons which branch out from the spinal cord and send impulses to muscles to allow them to be voluntarily controlled. Thus, when a motor neuron dies, it can no longer receive impulses from neurons in the brain and spinal cord and therefore cannot transmit impulses to muscle fibers. As more and more motor neurons die, fewer and fewer signals can be transmitted to the muscles. As the disease progress, the person will have difficulty moving his or her muscles, and these difficulties will only get worse as motor neurons continue to die, ultimately leading to complete paralysis.

When the muscles no longer receive impulses from motor neurons, they are not able to function and begin to break down, or atrophy. This deterioration contributes to decrease in strength, weight loss, gaunt-looking limbs, and eventual paralysis of muscles. ALS usually affects people between ages forty and sixty, but it can strike people of all ages.

The mechanics of ALS are analogous to many light bulbs in a room. The light switch is the brain, the wires are the motor neurons, and the light bulbs turning on are the muscles moving. If a single wire, a single motor neuron, is damaged and the switch is flipped, that one light bulb will not turn on, but the others will. Thus, the lighting of the entire room will not be affected very much; the person can still move. However, when many wires, many motor neurons, become damaged and the switch is flipped, the room will not be lit as brightly. Eventually, when all the wires are damaged, no matter how hard you flip the switch, the room will not light up. In people with ALS, as more and more motor neurons die, no matter how hard they try, they cannot move their muscles the way they want.

In 1869, Jean-Marie Charcot, a French neurologist, first noted ALS through a series of clinical observations and autopsies of patients. The name "amyotrophic lateral sclerosis" was not given to this disease until 1874 when Charcot's findings were printed in a collection called *Oeuvres Complètes*, a series of publications detailing Charcot's work. "Amyotrophic" literally translates to "no muscle nourishment." "Lateral" refers to motor neurons as they travel down the sides of the spinal cord, and "sclerosis" refers to the fact that the diseased neurons turn into hardened tissue after they die. Later, in 1939, ALS gained worldwide attention when renowned Yankee's baseball player Lou Gehrig came forward and stated he had this disease. ALS was later coined "Lou Gehrig's Disease."

People with a possible diagnosis of ALS may have a variety of symptoms depending on where in the body the motor neurons first begin to die. Some people first complain of weakness in a single arm or leg, while others notice it in the muscles involving speaking and swallowing, but in all cases, the weakness progressively gets worse and spreads to other body parts. With my dad, he would later tell me the first indication he knew something was wrong was when his golf swing just felt "off."

Muscle cramps are the other common complaint in addition to difficulties breathing as a result of the diaphragm getting weaker. Changes in speech and slurring of words occur as the muscles in the mouth and tongue begin to atrophy. Although I was initially not aware of it, my dad had all of these symptoms at the time of diagnosis, and they were magnified as he started to progress. The cramps were one of the first things that set my dad off, while my mom immediately noticed a slight change in his voice. Close friends would later tell us everyone thought he had had a stroke due to the difference in facial movements and the speech issues.

The pseudobulbular effect, which results in laughing or crying at inappropriate times, is also present in some. This aspect of ALS always made me chuckle. Before I knew he was sick, I will always remember the time we were watching some cute family movie with Matt Damon and Scarlett Johansson, and it had a cliché, happy ending. Kathryn and I couldn't help but smile at the end, but as I looked over, my dad was sobbing. This was a bit strange for me, as I had never seen my dad cry before. Ever. Not even when he got hit in the face with a piece of wood when helping set up for a gymnastics meet. Not even when our beloved neighbor died and my mom and I were sitting there bawling our eyes out. We just kind of stared at him and then chose to forget about it. I would later always joke with him about this instance and many others, including the oh-so-emotional *The Middle* on ABC. "I can't help it!" he would always insist. "It's just so funny!" The same would apply to any sad movie as well. While I was tearing up during *Zero Dark Thirty*, the last movie I ever watched with him, he was sobbing to the point he could barely catch his breath.

As ALS progresses even further, weakness in the muscles in the throat can cause choking, as the epiglottis, the flap that normally covers the opening to the windpipe when eating, cannot function properly. If fluids or food are aspirated, the person will have difficulties coughing up the foreign substance due to muscle weakness and breathing problems. Thus, choking is a huge problem in those with ALS. Muscle weakness in the mouth also causes eating to become very difficult, and the person can easily become malnourished and dehydrated. A feeding tube is often inserted into the stomach to deliver nutrients and fluids without the person having to take in food and water by mouth.

In addition to degrading the muscular system and affecting the person's ability to move, the respiratory system is greatly impacted. This is what affected my dad the most. The weakening of the diaphragm and intercostal muscles — the muscles between the ribs — greatly compromises the person's ability to breathe. The person can thus not receive enough oxygen, and carbon dioxide can build up quickly. The person will become extremely fatigued and will be especially susceptible to respiratory infections and pneumonia. Respiratory failure is often the cause of death in ALS patients. In end stages, a ventilator is often used to force air in and out of the lungs when the diaphragm can no longer function. The buildup of carbon dioxide is also common when the person cannot forcefully exhale enough. This is a fatal condition because carbon dioxide causes the blood to become acidic.

And what about that cough, the only indicator to me that my dad was sick? Well, the doctors have no idea. It is incredibly rare someone with ALS would have a dry cough as my dad did. There was no fluid or mucous building up in his lungs that he was trying to clear—he just had a "tickle" in his throat that wouldn't go away. He would eat cough drops by the dozen, and for some reason, still a mystery to the doctors, the cough would temporarily subside, possibly because the cough drops would numb his throat. The weird thing is, after months of coughing, just as suddenly as it appeared, one day he woke up and the cough was gone. No one knows why. Suddenly all those cough drops lying in odd places around the house had no use. However, as soon the cough disappeared, the other symptoms started showing up: the difficulty buttoning his shirt, the even slower speech, the problems breathing.

Despite all these symptoms of ALS, the sensory organs remain unaffected and a person's ability to think and reason is usually not impaired, although dementia is evident in five to ten percent of people with ALS. Even when paralysis eventually occurs, the person will still retain the sense of touch in all areas of the body because the sensory neurons are not damaged and can transmit impulses normally. A person's bowels and bladder also are rarely affected since these systems are controlled by a different part of the nervous system. In these ways, I have always said ALS is worse than being paralyzed due to a spinal cord injury, for example. In such cases, people cannot feel their legs nor can they move them, but with ALS, I could touch my dad—he could physically feel my hand on his foot or on his arm—and he wouldn't be able to move it the way he wanted to. In that way, ALS is truly like being trapped and locked in one's own body.

Like I've said, my dad's case was fairly unusual, with the weakness in his arms and legs progressing fairly slowly compared to his diaphragm. In fact, the day he died, he was still walking. On the other hand, you'll see people with ALS who have lived five, six, seven years and more and are confined to a wheelchair but have almost normal breathing measurements. It makes sense that they are still alive – after all, you can live without the use of your legs, but your diaphragm is awfully important – but doctors still do not understand these different progressions.

Due to the wide range of presentations of ALS from person to person, diagnosing ALS can often be difficult. Initial symptoms for my dad began in April 2012, and he was formally diagnosed just two months later in June. With most people though, the period from initial symptoms to diagnosis takes anywhere from ten to fourteen months. There is no definitive test to confirm ALS, so ruling out other diseases that have similar symptoms, such as multiple sclerosis (MS), Lyme disease, multifocal motor neuropathy, and other motor neuron diseases is a necessary first step. This tedious diagnosis process means people often have to see three or more specialists before ALS is ruled as the diagnosis. Delayed diagnosis can delay starting treatment and potential enrollment in clinical trials.

When looking to confirm a diagnosis of ALS, an electromyography (EMG) and a nerve conduction study (NCS) can test for electrical activity in muscles and nerves, respectively. Abnormalities in both these tests can suggest nerves and therefore, muscles are not functioning properly, a key factor involved in the diagnosis of ALS. MRI scans are also important to rule out other conditions, such as MS, a spinal tumor, or a herniated disk. A person with ALS will most likely have a seemingly normal MRI scan. Viruses and other conditions must also be ruled out by blood tests, and again, a person with ALS will be negative for these tests.

Around ninety percent of all cases of ALS are sporadic, meaning the cause is largely unknown, but many environmental factors have been suspected to be linked to

ALS. It is hypothesized that certain toxins such as heavy metals, solvents, radiation, and electromagnetic fields can result in ALS. Those with military experience, specifically veterans of World War Two, the Korean War, the Vietnam War, and the Gulf War, have been seen to have a higher rate of ALS. Football players and other people associated with high impact sports have also been seen to have a higher chance of developing ALS. In fact, retired NFL football players have been shown to have a four times than normal chance of developing ALS. In many cases though, as in with my dad, there is no clear cause of ALS.

On the other hand, around ten percent of ALS cases are genetic, in which case it is often called familial ALS (fALS). Certain genes, segments of DNA that code for proteins and make up who we are, may be mutated, meaning the DNA sequence has changed, which may cause ALS. Several genes have been identified so far that cause ALS when mutated such as SOD1, FUS, and C9ORF72, but researchers hypothesize there are many more genes that are yet to be associated with ALS. The most common inheritance pattern for these genes is autosomal dominant, meaning that only one copy of the mutated gene (from either parent) is required in order for the person to be affected by fALS. Thus, a person who has genetic ALS has a fifty percent chance of passing the mutated gene on to his or her children. Most of the time though, ALS is sporadic; genetic ALS is usually only indicated when there is a family history of ALS.

Unfortunately, there is currently no cure for ALS. Treatment of ALS mostly involves managing the symptoms. At this time, the only FDA approved treatment for ALS is a drug called Riluzole, which is licensed under the brand name Rilutek. This is the drug that caused my premature discovery of my dad's diagnosis, consequently leading to a three month long emotional rollercoaster. Riluzole works to protect neurons from being overexposed to glutamate, a neurotransmitter that often builds up in the spaces between neurons in people with ALS. Riluzole may slow the progression of the disease by a few months, but it cannot reverse damage that has already been done and is not a cure for ALS. In the case of my dad, it proved to be minimally effective. How ironic that it was what caused me to find out about his diagnosis.

* * * * *

I always like to think my family beats the odds and does better than what is expected. Both Kathryn and I consistently score in the ninety-eighth percentile for testing in school. My parents have both held positions in the workforce that were higher than most people. We live in a nice town in Maine that houses one of the top performing school systems in the state. And my mom is beating cancer, surprising her oncologists each day by simply being alive. It is nice to think that we are "exceptional," so it is no surprise that I believed my dad would live longer than the expected three to five years.

The day I found that bottle of medicine, the diagnosis did not make sense to me. He did not have any of the symptoms of ALS that I researched. He had a cough. That is what I kept telling myself. There was no way this diagnosis was correct. He had gone zip lining with me over the Texan desert just a few weeks before, tirelessly trudging through the hot and arid landscape without breaking a sweat. He played golf every single week and roughhoused with me in the backyard. If he had ALS, he could not have done any of those things.

But even if I did not want to admit it, my dad was sick. Rilutek has no other use other than for people with ALS.

That night, July 11th 2012, something inside of me changed. I went downstairs and began meticulously planning every single day of our trip to Paris in August, down to the hour. I wanted us to be able to see everything; this might be his last opportunity. I wanted it to be memorable, and I was determined to not leave room for any regret.

Chapter Three

In 1969 Elizabeth Kübler-Ross famously identified the five stages of grief: denial, anger, bargaining, depression, and acceptance. These stages may come in every order and may be accompanied by many other emotions as well.

I had cried myself to sleep the night I found the medication. I could not stop thinking about my dad. But when I woke up the next morning, I had forgotten all of these emotions. I wasn't even sad anymore because it didn't seem real. I kept repeating it over and over again: ALS, ALS, ALS. It seemed like a nightmare that was eating me alive and trapping me in this horrifying world of unknowns. But it wasn't.

A few days later I was on my mom's laptop trying to find an email about certain travel information, and when I opened her inbox, the first thing that popped up was a message to her friend. It was only eight words long, but those eight words confirmed that my life had been changed forever: "Hard day with confirmation of ALS in Boston."

I still didn't believe what I had read. If it was this bad, my parents would have told us. I did not want to approach them before they did. It had to be soon, right? They had always kept us in the loop, so why should this be any different? And so I waited. And waited. But several weeks had passed, and there was still no word on doctor's appointments or on a crazy disease called ALS.

Parents are the ones who guide children in life, even when their kids grow up and go to college and out into the real world. Parents are the ones their kids can count on to always be there. Having a terminally ill parent is unimaginable for most. But there can be things done to cope with the situation. You can ask questions and you can cry with them. You can talk to your friends and watch the casseroles pile up from complete strangers.

But for me, my parent was terminally ill and I couldn't tell anyone, because I wasn't supposed to know. This made me angry. It made me angry how my mom and dad wouldn't tell me about what was going on. It made me angry that I knew and they did not think I did. I became intolerant of the noise of his coughing. I wasn't angry or annoyed at him for coughing; I knew he couldn't help it. I was angry at the disease. I was angry that my dad was sick in the first place. Why him? Why now?

That summer I got to the point where I physically did not know how to cope with life anymore. I would be in the car and randomly start crying. When my mom would ask me what was wrong, I would say I was just tired. Gymnastics was my outlet, and when I was at the gym my mind was cleared of anything in the world of ALS. But when I wasn't at the gym, the emotions hurt too much. I began running and pushing myself to the point of near exhaustion. I craved the difficulty breathing that comes when you start climbing up a steep hill. I wanted to feel the kind of pain my dad was in. It wasn't fair that he was hurting and I wasn't. And in the end, every wave of anger plummeted into a wave of sobbing. I cried in the shower or silently at night, anyplace where no one would hear my cries of despair. I even scoped out a giant rock in the middle of the woods behind my house that I would run to so I could truly be alone with my tears. I began using food as a way to control all the things in my life that were beyond my own control. I ate oatmeal, yogurt, and chicken for virtually every meal because those were the things that made me happy. Then it came to a point where nothing made me happy anymore.

This was my bargaining: if I could make myself feel pain, then maybe, somehow, my dad wouldn't feel it as much.

I felt guilty for all the times I had ever been rude or inconsiderate to my dad. I vowed always to be pleasant around him and be the poster child for good behavior, because if I was a good daughter, then I reasoned, I might wake up and things would be different and he wouldn't be sick. But then the anger would flood over me again and I would suddenly lash out at him for coughing, leading to more guilt, and the cycle would continue.

Even things that should have made me happy made me sad. One warm summer night my mom built a fire in the backyard and the four of us sat around it, talking and having a good time. But suddenly I remembered that things would not be happy forever. My dad would soon not be able to talk anymore, or sit upright in a chair anymore, or breathe on his own anymore. My dad would no longer be the dad that I knew and loved. I started tearing up and told my parents I was tired, proceeding to go upstairs and sob alone in my bedroom.

* * * * *

Every time I looked at my dad, I knew that he would be gone soon, and that I was not supposed to know. I felt guilty for knowing, guilty for keeping this secret from my parents, the secret that made me question how to keep going on. I began posting on an ALS support group online forum. I described how I had found out my dad had ALS, but that my parents had not told me yet and how I was so overwhelmed with emotions, I didn't know what to do anymore.

The minute after I posted my first entry, I got three responses from complete strangers, telling me how much I was loved. Within a few hours, I had dozens. People were encouraging me to get off that website and talk to my parents, insisting they would not want me to be holding this secret all alone. I think that is what made me the most scared: I was alone in this situation. I know that sounds silly and that I could've told my parents at any point, but something inside of me was too scared to do that.

Reading through the posts made me jittery. I had been keeping this secret to myself and been in denial about it, but telling people, albeit complete strangers, made everything seem more real. The amount of "hugs" and thoughtful, warmhearted messages were so nice, but they made the tears come flowing all over again.

Initially, I didn't respond to any of the posts; I was too overwhelmed and scared. Then I watched as the posts came in from people who began to worry that I had not responded to anyone. There I was, a little fifteen-year-old girl who had just said she had this gigantic secret that her dad was going to die and who wasn't responding to anyone's messages, and yeah, I can see how they might've become a bit anxious that something had happened to me.

I tried to push the anger aside and make the rest of the summer as memorable as possible, but no matter how much I tried, I carried his illness with me wherever I went. I thought about it at every fleeting moment of the day. I could not push aside the fact that I knew he was going to die. It was almost as if I had contracted a disease as well, a disease that was preventing me from being happy in the face of my dad's illness. Indeed I had: depression.

* * * * *

The day my parents told me about my dad's illness was almost as memorable as the day I found out on my own. It was Tuesday, September 25th, 2012. My dad was helping me edit an essay for my civics class and he began having a coughing fit. He was always the kind of person who hated to admit defeat or give up, so even when he started coughing, he would always continue to talk. While he tried to talk to me about the history of *habeas corpus*, a cough interrupted every two words. I could feel the anger coming on, and I tried to hold it in, but I yelled at him.

I remember my words exactly, my tone of annoyance still echoing in my mind to this day: "Dad, go get a drink of water or go get one of your hundreds of cough drops that you have scattered throughout the house. But stop trying to talk while you're coughing."

Whenever I said something like that, dad would always ask me why I found him so annoying. I would always respond with something along the lines of "stop putting words into my mouth." This was not a new occurrence; I would frequently get angry at him about little things, particularly his coughing. It's truly not that I was annoyed — I knew he couldn't help it. I would always tell him I was only trying to help him and it made me angry when he didn't take care of himself. But that wasn't the real reason either. I was angry because he wouldn't tell us that he was sick. Even if I didn't know about the ALS, it was obvious that something was going on and that he and my mom were just pretending that everything was okay when it wasn't.

But this time when I lashed out at him, he got angry. "Give me break," he told me in a harsher-than-normal tone. I immediately backed off. I felt the guilt coming on. For the first time, I could sense his frustration.

After we finished looking through my essay, he told Kathryn and me that "Mom and Dad" had something they wanted to talk to us about. I groaned and gave the normal "stop talking in third person, we are not two years old" statement and then turned around in my chair at the kitchen counter.

The room was silent for a few moments, but then he began talking in a slow and quiet manner. His voice sounded different. He didn't even talk in third person. Once again, I remember exactly what he said: "So as you know, I've been going to see a lot of doctors recently, and I've been having lots of tests done. And Mom and I went down to Boston to see a neurologist. I have something called ALS."

That's all I remember word-for-word. After I heard the word ALS, I zoned out. Out of all the children whose mothers and fathers have sat them down and told them they have ALS—one of those "worst case scenario" diseases—I was probably the only one who breathed a sigh of relief. My secret was out. Finally. But then I could feel the anger coming on. I knew they had waited all that time for the right reasons. They were not trying to withhold any information from Kathryn and me; they only wanted us to be able to enjoy the summer before our innocence was taken away and our lives were changed forever. But my summer had already been tainted by this news, my innocence long gone.

My dad kept talking in his calm, and frankly strange, tone for another few minutes. Meanwhile, neither he nor my mom started to tear up. But I could feel the tears welling in my eyes. I didn't understand why I was crying; I already knew he was sick. I looked over at Kathryn. I could see her tears too. She had no idea. Then, as I wiped my eyes, in a blatant and forthright way I asked my dad what the life expectancy was.

"Well, we're hoping it will be a long time. Maybe ten years," my mom said. I laughed to myself. Yeah, sure. That was parent talk for "one percent of people with ALS live ten years after diagnosis, but we're hoping we're that one percent so we're going to say that." Like I said, I always like to think my family beats the odds. But in this case, how was I supposed to plan my life based on a one percent chance? What was I supposed to do if two years later I woke up and my dad wasn't here and I didn't get to live my life with him the way I wanted?

I didn't want to look at them. How was I supposed to break the news that I had known all along, and that ten years really wasn't what we most likely had? So, in a sassier tone than I had intended, I responded with, "Well, you're lucky. The average time is three to five years."

They both just stared at me. I couldn't imagine what was going through their minds. If they thought it would be a shock for us to hear that Dad was sick, well, I knew going in that the power of this little secret of mine would blow my parents away. "You knew," my mom said. The room went silent again.

"Well, of course I knew," I replied. Of course I knew. Even if I hadn't found that bottle of medication that day, I would have found out one way or another. Since that June day after the first doctor's appointment, I knew something had gone terribly wrong.

I expected my parents to look shocked, to become angry and interrogate me about how I knew, but they didn't. My mom asked how I knew and I told them I had found a bottle of medication. They didn't ask any more questions. I looked into their eyes, trying to figure out what they were thinking. There was something about having the power of this information against them that gave me the tiniest bit of pleasure. I know that sounds awful, but it was the one thing I was holding on to at that moment, the moment in which my world should have come falling down but didn't because it had already crashed two months ago.

Kathryn looked like she was about to explode trying to keep her tears in when finally she let loose and went and hugged my dad, burying her cheek into his shoulder. It was one of the only times I would ever see her cry like that. Both my mom and dad started to tear up, but I remained stoic. Angry.

Notice the common theme: anger. The anger consumed me. I was angry they hadn't told us until that night. I was angry my dad was sick. I was angry he wouldn't let us help him with anything. I was angry that I was so angry.

Soon after, the diagnosis once again started to become more real, the cycle of the "finding out" and subsequent grief starting all over again. I was forced to accept the subtle symptoms that I had kept pushing aside yet had gradually begun to notice: the slowness in speech, the tiredness, the moments when he would suddenly become out of breath. I was forced to accept this was the new reality. My secret was out, but for some reason I didn't feel any better. I felt worse. My dad was going to die.

* * * * *

The ensuing months were the darkest times of my life. On October 3rd, 2012, I fell down the stairs and suffered a concussion. At first the doctors didn't think it was that bad, but as the weeks passed, I just didn't get better. I was constantly in and out of school for months and I couldn't go to gymnastics. With nothing to do but sit at home with agonizing headaches and an increasing sense of life having no purpose, I was letting myself fall deeper and deeper into a hole of darkness that would prove incredibly difficult to pull myself out of. I didn't feel like eating and I spent more time crying than smiling. I just couldn't seem to remember how to be happy.

At school I tried to mask the sorrow on my face and put a patch over my aching heart, but my friends knew something was wrong. They just didn't know what. I didn't want to tell anyone that my dad was sick because I did not want anyone feeling bad for me.

I think the concussion was the "spark that ignited the flame" of my self-destruction. Once I could no longer exercise, attend school regularly, and continue on with my daily life, everything started to pile up. My dad's illness began to become even more real and I watched him grow worse and worse every day. The more upset I would get, the worse the headaches would become, which would in turn make me even more upset. It was a vicious cycle that ultimately drove me into the deep hole of depression.

Chapter Four

Remember all those commercials on TV about Cymbalta, with the narrator saying "Depression can hurt. Cymbalta can help?" I remember I used to watch these commercials and simply not understand why depression was a "thing." People get sad all the time. Sometimes you're tired and don't feel like doing anything. Why would you ever need medication for just feeling sad sometimes?

As I learned, however, depression is much more than simply feeling sad for a few days. I could go into the whole rant about how depression is a chemical imbalance in the brain and how it is an actual disease, but I think most people have heard this before. I had heard it before, but I still didn't understand why it was such a big deal. I don't think you can truly understand depression until you have experienced firsthand the powers of the beast. Looking back on these dark times in my life, I cannot even identify with the person I had become. I look frail and sad and lonely.

It was not getting out of bed one morning that was hard. It was getting out of bed *every* morning no matter how much sleep I got. Holding a simple conversation with someone took a tremendous amount of effort, and it just was easier for me to alienate myself from others.

One of my biggest frustrations was that my dad never wanted to accept help from anyone. He refused to see himself dwindling from the effects of ALS; to him, accepting help from someone meant announcing defeat. He was starting to choke on food a lot, and whenever he would start to choke, instead of asking for help or stopping to take a breath, he would continue talking and eating as if nothing was wrong. But that's the thing: it seemed as though *everything* was wrong. I could not put up with pretending that life was normal, because it wasn't.

As he struggled to do more and more, everything he did began to be accompanied by a sound effect of some sort, from a grunt to a sigh to a statement of, "I do not need any help." This perseverance was certainly admirable and embodied my dad's true spirit, but every time he choked or coughed or grunted as he tried to climb a flight of stairs was a constant reminder that he was sick, a constant reminder that our life was changing. And when I saw these constant reminders, I felt sad and sick to my stomach. Rather than trying to overcome these feelings of sadness, I found it easier, as I became accustomed, to isolate.

The basement in my house became my refuge. I could sit down there and watch TV or perhaps just stare at the wall, and no one would bother me. My sister was off doing her own thing and my mom was often caring for my dad. I found myself physically incapable of eating dinner with my family anymore because eating while watching my dad choke and struggle made me anxious and upset.

With my concussion recovery, my daily routine consisted of getting up at 6:30 a.m., making oatmeal for breakfast, sitting in the basement where I could be alone, going to school where I did the bare minimum required of me to get an A, going to lunch where I engaged in fake conversation with a smile plastered on my face, going to my last few classes, and waiting in the dark of the lobby where my dad would pick me up. Then I would go home, retreat to the basement, and usually fall asleep. If I was feeling well enough, around 4:30 p.m., I would go to gymnastics for an hour or so to do strength exercises, but I was mostly going there simply to say I went. When I started getting sad for no apparent reason, I would call my mom and have her pick me up. At home, I would yet again retreat to the basement and eat my dinner. Around 9:00 p.m. I would go upstairs, shower, and go to sleep. This pattern continued every day from October until March. I got to the point where I no longer felt sad; I felt nothing. I felt empty. I felt as though life no longer had a purpose.

If you'd asked many of my friends, they would have said that there was something a bit "off" with me, but that I had not necessarily isolated myself. Most people assumed it was just from the concussion that "wouldn't go away." Few people knew about my dad, and those few did not realize how affected by his diagnosis I was. After all, I would engage in conversations in class at school and joked around at lunch, and I was always involved with my teammates at gymnastics, going to every single one of their competitions.

But all of that was like watching the movie that Sarah Caldwell was putting on for everyone to see; most people did not know what was happening backstage. Backstage I was hurting so badly, to the point that one night I buried myself in a snow bank in attempt to feel something. I was not engaging in conversations and joking around at lunch because it came naturally to me; I was acting, trying to appear normal, as if nothing was wrong.

At gymnastics meets, I was smiling and cheering on my teammates because it was the right thing to do, but backstage I was watching in agony and jealousy, stuck on the sidelines, unable to compete. At the same time, I could not even picture myself doing gymnastics anymore because I no longer found joy in it. I no longer found joy in most things that I once loved. Sometimes really sick people reach the point where nothing in life seems to matter anymore. Well, I had reached that point. Even to this day, I don't think many people knew how bad off I really was.

The thing is, people didn't know because I didn't want to tell them. I thought if I kept my emotional agony to myself it would hurt less, because I wouldn't need to explain that my dad had a disease and he was going to die; I wouldn't have to see the looks on peoples' faces as I broke the news, as they suddenly saw me as a different person, a person who had a sick father. Besides, why did anyone need to know? No one could say anything that would make everything okay, because it would not be okay. My dad was going to die and there was nothing anyone could do. No one understood what I was going through. No one else was watching their father dying right before their eyes.

No one could possibly understand how I felt angry more than I felt sad, how I resented my dad every time he coughed. They couldn't understand why I wanted my dad just to die already. I didn't even know why I wanted this, because every time I thought it, I told myself I was a terrible person for thinking this way. I knew I needed to treasure the moments I spent with my dad, but sometimes it was just too hard to feel sad, to channel my emotions, and anger was an easier way out. Because if I kept being angry that my dad was sick, then I wouldn't have to deal with being sad. I was tired of crying.

I thought that if I told people how I was feeling, I would become "that" person they would look at and say, "Wow, I'm really glad I'm not her." Because quite honestly, being sixteen years old and knowing your dad is going to die really sucks. And I didn't think anyone else got that, so why should I have to tell anyone how I was feeling?

I don't like to make mistakes. I mean, no one does. But I made three major mistakes in these months that all people can learn from.

Big Mistake Number One: thinking that isolation would somehow make the emotions go away. The longer I waited to tell anyone, the harder it got to try to bring it up. Even my best friends never really saw my dad, so they wouldn't have known anything was wrong. Yet no matter how many times I was going to bring it up, every time I told myself it wasn't the "right" time. Well, there is no *right* time to break this kind of news. Every time I told myself I wasn't ready for the "I'm sorries" and "Let me know if there's anything I can do to helps" because a) yeah, well why wouldn't you be sorry, everyone is, but you have no idea what it's like; and b) no, you can't do anything. ALS has no cure and my dad is going to die. But the truth was, I would never be ready for any of this, because every time is the wrong time to tell someone your dad is going to die.

So as you can imagine, I was trapped in a vicious cycle. The longer I held it in, the easier it became to keep it to myself, but the harder it became to wake up every day and not feel angry, to wake up and see that there is a purpose to life.

For some reason, one day when I met a friend for coffee at Starbucks, I decided to tell her. I hadn't talked to this girl in a while because we didn't see each other much at school, but something inside of me said to tell her. Maybe it was easier because I knew Olivia wasn't the type of person to start freaking out or to become overly emotional, or maybe it was because I hadn't talked to her in a while and bringing this up out of the blue seemed a bit easier. Whatever the case, something told me that although this moment still wasn't the "right" one, it was going to have to be okay.

I was prepared for the "Oh my goodness I'm so sorry," that I had imagined as I said I had something to tell her, that my dad had this disease called ALS and was going to die in the next few years, as I started to hyperventilate and try to prevent the tears from falling in front of all those people at Starbucks. What were you supposed to say in a situation like that? Even I could not articulate the "perfect" response, because there really is nothing you can say.

In that moment, sitting at a table across from this girl with a hot cappuccino in my hands, I realized that all the ideas I had carried for months about needing to isolate because I thought no one could understand or do anything about my dad's illness had led only to greater suffering. I came to understand that sometimes all a person needs — all I needed right then — was to be able to talk. That is exactly what Olivia let me do. I could see it in her eyes — the shock, the concern — but she didn't try to sugarcoat it. She didn't ask many questions or go on a long rant about how "everything happens for a reason." She just let me talk.

I talked about how I found out my dad was sick through finding his medication and how I hadn't told anyone for months and how I hadn't told anyone even after my parents officially told my sister and me, about how he was eventually going to lose the ability to walk and talk and eat and breathe. But not once did I talk about how I was feeling, because I wasn't ready. In the eyes of a psychiatrist or some other mental health expert, was it the "healthiest" decision on my part to keep my emotions in? Maybe not, but I had been at it for the past five months, and it was the only way I knew.

I left Starbucks that day feeling a bit lighter, a bit more able to live my life. I felt relieved and wondered why I hadn't told anyone before. I felt like I owed it to other people to tell them what was going on, but the more I reflected on that afternoon with Olivia, the less I wanted to relive that experience. I didn't want to have to explain myself, to start hyperventilating and crying all over again.

A month went by before I finally told someone else. I was at my friend Grace's house right after Christmas when I told the story all over again. Somehow it was a bit easier this time; I had been through it before. But as expected, the tears still fell down my face, and they fell down Grace's too. I thought seeing her cry would make me even sadder, but it made me smile. Maybe she didn't understand firsthand what was going on, but she "got" how bad it was.

So this brings me to Big Mistake Number Two: refusing to tell people my dad was sick simply because I was afraid of their reaction. I thought people would just feel bad for me but wouldn't really care, because many of my friends didn't know my dad all that well. I wished he had been the soccer coach that everyone loved or the cool dad that everyone always wanted to say "hi" to at the grocery store, anything that would maybe make people want to care a bit more. I thought that tears would mean they felt bad for me, that they were just glad they weren't in my situation.

We as humans have an incredible ability to connect with others. We *want* to feel what others are feeling, so when you see a person crying, you want to cry too, no matter what they are crying about. That night I realized that when someone cried when I told them my dad was sick, it wasn't that they were crying for me or that they were feeling bad for me; they were crying *with* me. Grace knew my dad, but it didn't matter if she did or not. I could have told her about my uncle or a family friend or anyone, and seeing me upset would still have made her upset. I thought seeing the emotion in other peoples' eyes, the outpouring of love and support and hugs would make it harder; I thought it would be annoying, because after all, this was *my* dad, not theirs. But I was wrong. People crying alongside me made it easier, easier to finally open myself up to someone.

When she asked me if I was okay, I wanted to respond with the "Yeah, I'm fine" answer that I had planned, but I held back. "I'm really sad," I told her. I put down my defensive shield for that one moment because I wasn't okay, and I owed it to her to tell her.

Big Mistake Number Three: thinking that people would know how I was feeling just because I told them my dad was sick. After all, as I keep saying, no one else knew what it was like for me. No one else understood my situation, so why should they know how I was feeling? How was anyone supposed to know if I was fine or not fine, sad or angry, depressed or in denial, unless I told them? As it turned out, I felt a whole mix of emotions that I don't even understand today. But I do know that talking about them can help. I was not okay, but maybe telling Grace that I was sad was a first step toward my being at least a little bit better.And at that point, it was the biggest step I could take. Speaking openly about my feelings might have been a step in the right direction, but it proved to be a direction I was still unwilling to go.

Which led me to, finally, Big Mistake Number Four: repression of emotions. We all do it. When someone asks in casual conversation, "How are you?" you respond with "Good, thanks." It's never "Actually, I'm having a crappy day," because oftentimes people simply don't want to hear that. I don't care how perfect your life is, "good" is not a sufficient answer. Maybe you really are "good" as in you're having a great day, but there's something that's bothering you, something that isn't quite "perfect." After my dad got sick, if someone had asked me how I was and I had responded truthfully, I would've said something along the lines of, "Well, actually life kind of sucks. My dad is going to die, I'm always angry, I cry a lot, and I wake up every morning feeling like there is no purpose in life, so yeah, not so good." While this might not be the appropriate answer when talking to your dentist, when someone you're close to asks you that, it's how you're supposed to answer.

Telling my friends about my dad gave me even more opportunities to talk about how sad I was, how angry I was, but I still refused to open up. In fact, the more people I told, the more emotionless I became whenever I talked about my dad, because it was simply the easiest direction to take. Reciting the same script over and over again, saying how my dad had ALS and was probably going to die in a few years, seemed to be so much easier when tears didn't get in the way.

Life lesson of the moment: the right way is oftentimes not the easy way, but it is worth the extra push. The more I said I was "good" and "fine," the more I believed it, and the less I would be willing to talk about anything related to how I was feeling. It was an endless cycle that could have been largely prevented if I had just been willing to talk to someone, to anyone, for *real*.

My mom saw me getting worse and worse, but I still refused to open up even to her. Moms have a funny way of just knowing things about their child, and although I never told her, she knew. She knew how sick I had gotten, and she did everything in her power to pull me out of the hole that I had dug for myself. My mom is one of those moms that everyone likes. She is the one that all my friends go up to and hug, and she gives them an even bigger hug back. She is the one who will snuggle me at night and lie with me until I fall asleep. She is the one who is always reminding me that she is my number one fan and that she would do anything for me. She is the one who loves me more than I can even imagine. Yet I did not do a good job at loving her back, at accepting her help, because I didn't even want to talk to her. I didn't want to talk about all that was going on because I didn't know that it was okay for me to feel so angry, to feel resentment toward my dad, to want him to die already, and I didn't want to admit this even to my mom.

It wasn't as though my dad was an inconvenience — I would have done anything for him — it's that the disease itself was an inconvenience. It was an inconvenience for every sentence to be interrupted by a cough, an inconvenience for life not to be *normal*. Whenever I had these feelings, I would tell myself how much of a bad person I was for wanting my dad to die, to think of him as annoying, because I knew he couldn't help it. And with these feelings of guilt, I was driven into more sadness and in turn more anger, and the cycle once again would continue.

As I would tell it, around February my mom and the concussion doctor *"forced* me to see a mental doctor for all of my problems." This meant I would need to talk about all my feelings and talk about ALS and my dad and the concussion to yet another person, another person who would try to be all cheerful and give another version of the "we're really concerned about you" speech that I had heard from my mom and my concussion doctor. So I walked into the psychiatrist's office, a small boxed off room in my pediatrician's office that had mahogany finished everything, put a smile on my face and said I was "fine." I said my dad had ALS and was getting worse and that I was recovering from a concussion that wouldn't go away, and yes, sometimes I got sad, but that's normal, right?

I don't know how she did it, but this doctor saw right through me. Just by talking to me for five minutes, she saw that I was not fine. I mean I guess she was a professional and all, but I thought I had done a pretty good job of giving a convincing story of how "fine" I was. Looking back, I don't know why I ever would have done that. I was going to see a doctor — someone who could help me — and I had still refused to say how I was truly feeling. They say the first step is admitting you have a problem, and I guess in her office that day I admitted, albeit to myself, that it was an issue, the way I was living. She got down on my level and I somehow connected to her, listening to what she was saying. She told me it can be scary to have a sick parent and that I might have weird emotions that I couldn't explain, from extreme sadness to anger.

She said it. Anger. Someone got it. Someone finally got it. She said it was okay to be feeling however I felt, because there was no wrong answer to anything. She told me I couldn't control how I was feeling, and sometimes there is no explanation as to why I was feeling a certain way. I think this was the key message to me: it was okay that I was feeling the way I was. Maybe she didn't have personal experience with what I was feeling — I have no idea what her life has entailed — but she nevertheless understood me. Despite this, I still wasn't ready to actually "talk about my feelings" in a true and honest way, so I didn't say much back. She said that was okay. She didn't push me and didn't try to pry answers out of me. We just talked.

She ended up prescribing a certain type of medication that she thought might help me. When she first mentioned this, I told myself I would refuse to take them. I was not crazy or insane and I didn't need to be jacked up on "happy pills" that would make me happy when I really wasn't. But then she described how they would work.

Depression is a physical condition, not just a "crazy person" disease. It is often caused when serotonin, a neurotransmitter that helps moderate mood, sleep, memory, and appetite, is not being transmitted correctly between neurons in the brain. The medication I was put on worked to increase the levels of serotonin in my brain by preventing serotonin from being reabsorbed after it was released into the space between neurons in the brain. This allowed messages in my brain to be transmitted for a longer period of time. Thus, in theory, when I experienced an event that would normally make me feel happy, I would be able to fully experience this happiness rather than a feeling of sadness or discontent. It wouldn't suddenly make me feel happy; rather, it would make coping with difficult situations in life easier and my innate happiness to come out.

This medication did not magically work overnight, nor did it simply "fix" me. I knew if I wanted to get better I needed to empty my brain of all the "baggage" of emotions that had been hanging out since July when I found out my dad was sick. The problem was, I didn't know how to start. I started seeing a social worker whom I talked with on a regular basis, but I still couldn't break down the barrier and show my true self. I didn't want to be vulnerable, to admit how I truly felt, because although I knew it wasn't "wrong" per se, what was the point? I knew how to live life trapped in an emotionless bubble, and I didn't want this bubble to pop suddenly. I needed something else to do it for me.

That something came when we were on a family vacation in Grand Cayman for spring break. For the first time, my dad's illness became "real." For the first time, I truly saw his pain as he struggled to do things that he was once able to do.

* * * * *

It was April 2013. Ten months earlier, my dad had been diagnosed with ALS. As he was getting into the car to go to the airport, his legs suddenly went limp and dangled behind him as he tried to crawl across the seat. My grandma was with us, and for the first time, she too, saw how weak he had become. She started quietly crying. I remember thinking my dad looked like a fish out of water. He initially pushed aside any offers from us to help him, but once it became evident that he could not move in the way he had intended, I pulled him up and into the seat. He was exhausted and breathing very heavily, just from those few seconds of trying to get into a car. I just watched as he closed his eyes, silently crying to himself inside. Within moments he looked normal again, but I couldn't get this image out of my mind: the frustration, the embarrassment on his face from not being able to get into a car.

At the airport, he navigated pretty well and refused to get pushed in a wheelchair alongside my grandma. But when we got to the island, there was a short walk from where the plane landed to the airport building. He still refused a wheelchair, shuffling his way alongside us in the eighty-five degree heat. Then, when we got inside, he started coughing. And he couldn't stop. I realized how tired he was, how the heat and a three minute walk could tire his lungs this much and instigate such an awful coughing spell. From that instance, I don't know if he ever truly recovered during the trip. We got to the condo and he went straight to sleep and I didn't see him for several hours. He went to dinner with us, but then he went to sleep again. The next morning, he woke up, watched golf on TV (the Master's was on, a very big deal!), and then went down to the beach for an hour.

Whenever my dad sat on the beach, he always stationed himself under the umbrella in the shade, reading a self-help book about "how to be a better person" or "how to succeed in business and make people like you more." But this trip was a bit different. He didn't take any books with him at all. That day he just sat under the umbrella and stared at the water. When he got tired, we brought him back up to the condo and he took a nap, eventually waking to watch more golf and eat a small lunch before falling back asleep before dinner. And this was the routine that he fell into.

Then one day my mom and I decided we were going to get him in the water. The sand was hot and uneven, making it difficult for him to balance, so after initial resistance, we finally got him to agree to go down to the water. My mom took one arm and I took the other, and we slowly walked him down. As we did this, I knew other people were watching. I knew other people were wondering what was wrong with him. I knew they were inevitably feeling sorry for us. They were glad their teenage daughter did not have to help her dad walk.

But you know what? I was glad I had this opportunity, this opportunity to help my dad in any way possible. When we got to the water, his legs were too weak to support him and he couldn't stand alone as the gentle waves bumped up against him. We got him up to his waist and my mom and I held him tightly as the waves washed up against us. I saw a subtle smile emerge on his face. He was in the ocean. It may not seem like a huge deal, but for him, it was a refusal to give up. For me, it was the beginning of my doing everything I could to help my dad live the life that he wanted to.

My mom took a picture of my dad and me after we got out of the water. To this day, that is one of the pictures I will always cherish the most. My dad is smiling, and I am smiling — for real. Behind both our smiles is some pain; after all, how could there not be? But those smiles tell our story. They tell the story of refusing to give up. My dad once told me that he would not stop doing anything until he absolutely could not do it anymore. He was the epitome of someone who would never give up. But even as this disease challenged him in ways he could never have imagined, I was determined to help him still do the things he loved.

While in Grand Cayman, we went on a boat to go snorkeling. It was in Grand Cayman many years prior that my dad had taught me how to snorkel. He taught me how to breathe through the tube and how to dive down and squirt water out of the tube when I surfaced again. It was in Grand Cayman when I was seven years old that he dove thirty feet down into the coral reef to get a conch shell for me, which I still have to this day.

Seeing him on the boat, alone, as we were all in the water made my heart break. I knew his heart was breaking too, more than I could ever know, but there was nothing I could do. He no longer had the strength to swim in deep waters — the irony being that he was the one who taught me how to swim in the first place. Now I was in the deep waters of the ocean and he was back on the boat.

But then we went to a sandbar to see stingrays. These stingrays were incredibly friendly and the water was only waist deep. However, getting on and off the boat can be challenging, especially when using a small metal ladder. And as before, even the slightest wave would knock my dad over, and the waves on the sandbar were stronger than back on the beach. Even my dad became a bit skeptical about his abilities, and he almost didn't go in. But I insisted. With the help of one of the crewmembers, we lifted him into the water and grabbed onto his arm as he waded through the water. He couldn't scuba dive or snorkel, but he sure could get up close and personal with these marvelous creatures. The stingrays brushed up against my dad's feet, tickling him in search of food, and he held one between his thin arms. It was almost as if everything was normal. In a way, it was. It was the first time I came to terms with the fact that this indeed was normal, my first shot at acceptance. It was our *new* normal.

In the airport on our way back home, we were forced to get a wheelchair for my dad due to the long distances between gates. It was the first time he ever had to be pushed around, and I remember looking at him and thinking he was going to cry. "I don't like this, Sarah," he told me.

"I know, Dad. I know." To this day, I can still see that look on his face. It was the beginning of a rapid decline due to ALS. And there were no hopes of getting better.

After this trip, however, it didn't matter to me anymore that things were no longer "normal" and that my dad needed some extra help. I was willing to do anything to put a smile on his face. And the smile on my face was no longer made of plaster; it was real. I was a new person with a new outlook on life. Not only was I happier, I was more armed to cope with my dad's progressing illness and maintain a relatively positive perspective on life. It sounds like an oxymoron, but I was happier because I had finally recognized how sad I was that my dad was sick. In just admitting this to myself, the anger began to lessen every time he coughed or needed help getting a glass of water, the sadness starting to disappear as I was finally able to begin the process of literally picking myself up off the ground. I was reaching a point, in some ways, of acceptance, acceptance that my dad was sick.

Do I wish I had been able to do this sooner, to recognize that I would only ever truly be happy again if I first admitted to myself how angry and sad I always was? Absolutely. I would love to have gotten off the roller coaster of emotions months earlier, but it's easy to say you would have done things differently once you already know what will happen. Before this trip, I simply did not have the tools to be able to get off that roller coaster. If I found myself in the same situation again, there's no saying that I would act any differently. And that's okay, because, as I have been told over and over again, it's okay to feel the way you do. For me, once I dug myself into that hole, it was hard to get out, and it is like that for many people, but not all.

Maybe after the trip it was easier for me because my dad was finally admitting that he *did* need help sometimes and that he couldn't keep trying to do things on his own. It was the definition of his view on life to keep going even when things get tough, but when he chose to walk across the room to get a glass of water and then was unable to walk up the stairs to get to his bed, that is when the expenditure of energy just wasn't worth the effort.

I know it sounds selfish, that life seemed to be easier once my dad started getting worse. The start of his calling for help was undoubtedly one of the hardest transformations for him. He always used to tell me that *he* was the one who was supposed to be caring for *me*, not the other way around. Asking for help from his daughter, in his eyes, was reversing the roles; I was the one now taking care of him. But that was okay. And I began to tell him that often. I began to tell him I loved taking care of him, because it was true. And this never would have been the case even just a few weeks before.

* * * * *

This was my new way of thinking. This life was our new normal. And despite my dad getting worse every day, I was happier than I had ever been. I was happier because I had embraced how I was truly feeling. I talked more openly to my mom and my friends, and I even let the tears come out with my social worker. I was happier because I had accepted our new normal.

But then again, what really is *normal*? Is it sitting at the dinner table and talking about what everyone did that day, trying to stretch the time and reach that goal of a thirty-minute long dinner? Because I remember when we would do this, before my dad was sick, and Kathryn and I would just sit there, counting down the minutes until we could go do something else less boring. So is normal trudging together through the snowy woods as a family to cut down a Christmas tree every year? Because I remember that too, my parents dragging us along every year except the last, Kathryn and I throwing tantrums every time because we were cold or tired or hungry.

When my dad got sick, our *normal* changed. As he got progressively worse we needed to make changes in our lives in order to accommodate his needs. Yet, I still had two loving parents and a wonderful sister, all who would risk their lives to help me. I still lived in a welcoming home and had amazing friends.

Sure, there were some changes here and there, and it's no secret that I missed our old life in many ways. Maybe my dad could no longer wrestle with me and play "stuck forever" like we used to when I was little, but in the end, he was still a person, a husband, a friend, not just some guy with ALS. He was my dad. He would still flip out whenever a road or an appliance or whatnot was "poorly designed," and he still would be a cheapskate and want to buy the knock off version of something over the "good" kind. He would still come into my room at 10:00 p.m. and tell me it was getting late and it was "night nights," even though I was a teenager and, as I would tell him, "I clearly know what time it is."

While once these little annoyances just contributed to how uncool my dad was, they were what ultimately allowed me to form an even tighter connection with him. These little things reminded me that my dad was indeed still the person he used to be and he was fighting with all his might to stay that way. He was struggling just to walk, yet he would make the point to walk to my room to say goodnight and remind me that I needed sleep. He was struggling just to talk, yet he would still ask me questions that he already knew the answer to, simply to fill the conversation and connect with me.

I once found my dad's constant chatter and other little flaws obnoxious and I yearned for those few weeks a year when my dad would be away for business or a scuba diving trip. I looked forward to Tuesday nights when he played golf and we could have "girl time" at home. I remember thinking that life would be so much easier if my dad were gone all the time. I thought I would fight less with my mom and my sister and life would be more peaceful and enjoyable in general. Well, as they always say, be careful what you wish for. Because as I am sitting here, less than a year after my dad was taken away from me, I honestly would give anything to talk with him just one more time. I wish I could just hear his voice one more time and tell him, just one last time, how much I loved him.

Chapter Five

Going into Summer 2013, I knew my dad was getting worse. He was no longer on the "five to seven year plan" that we had initially thought. He was no longer beating the odds.

He was having increased difficulty breathing and he couldn't walk long distances. He spent most of the time either in the living room propped up in his favorite chair or in his bedroom where it was air-conditioned. Every move that he made was accompanied by a sound effect of some sort—usually a grunt—and while sounds like that would have once bothered me, they no longer did. I knew he was suffering, and I hated seeing him like that.

He got a machine called a BiPAP, which helped him breathe by forcing air in and out of his lungs. At night he would wear a mask that was attached to this machine, and it seemed to give him some relief and help him breathe better. This machine was one of the big steps in my dad's ALS journey; it was the first "special device" that he had to use as a result of his disability. However, he didn't fight this one; he recognized how much it was helping him, especially when he was so tired and had a hard time catching his breath just by standing up.

When I went to Paris with my dad in August 2012, we walked up the Eiffel Tower. This is no easy feat for a normal person (there are 704 steps that go up at an increasingly steep angle), let alone a person with early stage ALS. But he made it. Looking back, I have no idea how he did it with such grace and defiance; at that point, he didn't know I knew he was sick, and he did not complain once about being weak or tired. If I hadn't known any better, I would have said he was completely healthy, barely breaking a sweat when we got to the top. However, the energy it took my dad to climb to the top would have been equivalent to me strapping a 100-pound weight belt to my chest and running up the stairs as fast as I could. That was at the beginning of his battle with ALS.

Six months later, in early 2013, walking up a one-story flight of stairs to his bedroom was a struggle, but he kept doing it because, as he would always tell me, "I'm not going to stop doing anything until I absolutely cannot do it anymore."

Try sprinting up the stairs with that one hundred pound weight belt strapped to your chest and do that ten times. That is the amount of energy it took my dad to walk up the stairs just one time. Another six months later, in Summer 2013, it had come to the point where he physically couldn't do it anymore (think 300-pound weight belt). It's no surprise we soon had a "stair chair" put in to help him get up and down. It's hard to believe that just one year before he had been walking up the Eiffel Tower. Now he could barely walk a few steps without being winded. That is how fast his illness progressed.

My dad was incredibly resistant to getting that stair chair. Even that summer he insisted he could climb the stairs no problem, but we knew he couldn't go on like that much longer. I can still picture him stumbling up those stairs like it was yesterday: his back hunched over, his arms clinging to the railing, shaking, and trying to pull himself up the stairs inch by inch, step by step, the frightful sounds coming from him as he gasped for air the entire time.

The whole process took around five minutes or so, and by the time he got to the top, he could barely walk anymore because he was so tired. My parents' bedroom is on the second floor, so whenever my dad wanted to go lie in bed, he would have to use a tremendous amount of energy. It's ironic, isn't it, that he would have to struggle and make himself even more exhausted in order to go rest from being tired in the first place.

A few months earlier, seeing that stair chair would have caused me to spiral into a period of even more intense depression and anger. It was an ugly contraption and every time I walked up the stairs it was in my way, a constant reminder my dad was sick. It was even in my dog's way: he could no longer sleep at the base of the stairs because the rail took up too much space. But in fact, I encouraged my dad to get the stair chair. I could not bear seeing him try to climb the stairs anymore; it was a colossal waste of his energy. He could have used that energy to do more important things, like going to Kathryn's basketball game or eating dinner with us.

But those family dinners were becoming a thing of the past. He gradually came to eat less and less, and often would just sit at the dinner table and say a few words here and there. I began to feel incredibly guilty for all those times I had refused to eat dinner with my family because I could not "emotionally handle it." It sounds pathetic now, I know, and while at the time it was incredibly difficult for me, I would give anything to go back in time and change the way I handled things. I had always wished that we could be one of those families that didn't have to have a family dinner every single night, yet another instance of "be careful what you wish for," because now I could only dream of the four of us sitting down together for dinner.

Eventually, rather than forcing himself to consume small calorie-packed meals that he would have to eat every hour, struggling through the coughing and choking, my dad got a feeding tube that allowed him to receive the nutrients he needed and to maintain his weight, which had been shrinking by the day. The feeding tube was one of those "steps" in his deterioration; it truly signified the transition to a state where my dad was dependent on others for the most basic things, like eating — or in this case, getting nutrients. A feeding tube is essentially an external tube that is inserted into the stomach during a minor surgical procedure. The tube provides a way for food to reach the stomach without having to be chewed up and swallowed, something that was becoming more difficult for my dad every day.

The stuff that we put into the tube wasn't really food though — it was liquid nutrition from a can that packed as many calories as possible into a small volume of liquid, a cream colored, chalky substance that my dad would always make a face at when we put it in the tube. I would laugh every time, trying to lighten the mood — although his face really did look funny. Seriously though, I didn't blame him. That stuff was disgusting, and to make matters worse, the first ingredient was corn syrup. Delicious.

While it was nice that we no longer had to force my dad to eat when he wasn't hungry, the biggest part of it all was that he was no longer at risk for choking. I'll always remember the time when we were in Boston and went out to dinner one night at a small restaurant. The weather had been hot, which made breathing harder for my dad. Some nights instead of going to dinner he just stayed in the hotel room where it was cool, but this one night was a bit cooler than the others, so he decided to eat something and skip the canned nutrition and feeding tube for the night. We sat outside because we knew he always enjoyed sitting outside for dinner, and he ordered salmon, his favorite meal. It came out and looked wonderful. I could see him starting to get excited. He had lost his taste for most food because it was getting harder and harder for him to eat, but we knew this salmon would be good for him because it was so moist and would be easy for him to swallow.

But upon the first bite, he started choking. And he just couldn't stop. The muscles in his throat were too weak to cover his windpipe as he ate, so food could easily get stuck, essentially causing him to aspirate it. Coughing normally cleared the food from his lungs, but his chest muscles were just too weak; as much as he coughed, it would not get out. We sat there for fifteen minutes and watched in agony as he tried to catch his breath. We knew he would have to keep coughing until the piece came up and he could catch his breath. But we didn't know if he would ever catch his breath. We didn't know what we could do to stop his choking. The answer? Nothing. We didn't know what we could do to stop his ALS. The answer to that? Nothing as well.

After half an hour or so we sat him in his wheelchair and wheeled him across the street to the hotel. We put him on the BiPAP and watched as he slowly breathed in air from the mask. An hour later he had stopped coughing. But he was exhausted and could barely move.

After that, any time I ever asked him if he wanted to go someplace or do something and he would tell me how tired he was, and I would always say to him, "I know," in the most sympathetic way possible. But the trouble was, I, like most people, truly had no idea what it was like for my dad to live with ALS. Sure, I could watch the suffering and the agony, and I could be scared for him and with him, but I had no idea what it was like for him to be choking that one night. I was scared, but I cannot imagine how scared he must have been. People cannot truly understand the beast of this disease until they have walked in the shoes of someone who has it. I imagine what my dad was going through that night would have been somewhere along the lines of choking on a piece of food from eating too quickly and trying to cough it up and catch your breath, all while breathing through a straw and running a mile. But at the same time, I truly have no idea what it was like.

While describing the everyday challenges a person with ALS faces, from buttoning their shirt to signing their name, former New Orleans Saints football player Steve Gleason, who was diagnosed with ALS in 2011, used the analogy of trying to floss your teeth while being trapped headfirst in a sleeping bag. My dad had always been a big talker, and the harder it got for him to talk, the less he was able to say. Try putting two large marshmallows in your mouth and having a long conversation. That's the effort required to say just a few words. No wonder a speech-generating device on his iPad was soon necessary for my dad. It was bad enough for him that he needed help getting dressed, walking (or riding) up the stairs, and eating (or receiving canned nutrition), but then ALS began to rob him of the thing that defined him most: his voice.

I used to say how annoying it was when my dad would talk all the time. He would always want to know the most miniscule details about everything in my life, and he would ask question after question after question. He loved to tell a story about "back when I was a kid" and how he didn't have a car when he was a teenager, so therefore I shouldn't get a car. He would always talk to my friends but somehow forget their names or ask some dumb question ("So how's math class going this year?") and I would think he was the most embarrassing dad I had ever met. I used to wish he wouldn't talk as much. And here it comes again: be careful what you wish for. I would give anything to hear my dad's voice just one more time, to hear him ask me a boring question about how my day. I would give anything to have one more conversation over a family dinner.

* * * * *

Several years before he was diagnosed with ALS, my mom, Kathryn, and I helped put on a surprise fiftieth birthday party for him. While going through old boxes, preparing to make a bunch of posters with pictures from my dad's life, I came across a newspaper clipping that my grandmother had once given me. I'm not sure where it came from or who wrote it (there's no author), so I'm just going to say it is anonymous. Here is how it goes:

FATHER
4 Years: My daddy can do anything.
7 Years: My dad knows a lot, a whole lot.
8 Years: My father doesn't know quite everything.
12 Years: Oh, well, naturally Father doesn't know that, either.
14 Years: Father? Hopelessly old-fashioned.
21 Years: Oh, that man is out-of-date. What did you expect?
25 Years: He knows a little bit about it, but not much.
30 Years: Maybe we ought to find out what Dad thinks.
35 Years: A little patience. Let's get Dad's assessment before we do anything.
50 Years: I wonder what Dad would have thought about that. He was pretty smart.
60 Years: My dad knew absolutely everything!
65 Years: I'd give anything if Dad were here so I could talk this over with him. I really miss that man.

At age ten, I truly was in between the stage of "My father doesn't quite know everything" and "Oh, well, naturally Father doesn't know that either." I thought my dad was kind of weird sometimes, but I still thought he was pretty cool. But by age fourteen, my dad was not only "hopelessly old-fashioned" but also incredibly annoying and by far the most un-cool dad around. However, by age fifteen, when I knew he was sick, I skipped ahead a few years, because although the "patience" with him was initially slower to come, at that point my school of thought was always "Let's get Dad's assessment before we do anything." No matter how annoyed or angry with him (and this disease) I was, I still found myself always seeking him out for advice.

I remember when I was ten years old I started tearing up when I first read this little article. At the time, I was not someone who would tear up easily (although that has certainly changed now). There was something about that last line though, the line of the 65-year-old: "I'd give anything if Dad were here so I could talk this over with him. I really miss that man." No matter how much I thought my dad was a bit weird, I could not imagine myself without my dad, even at age sixty-five.

Little did I know I would find myself feeling this at age sixteen. I had somehow aged forty-nine years overnight. This article indicates that my dad was taken away from me thirty-four years before he was supposed to be. It indicates that people my age *should* think their dad is annoying and embarrassing. I remember finding this article shortly after he died and starting to sob because it wasn't fair that he was gone. It wasn't fair that, at age fifty-six he was dead yet my grandpa was still alive. I should have still been thinking that my dad was "useless" and didn't know anything.

But I wasn't. And I never would again. My dad "knew absolutely everything" and was "pretty smart" (well, extremely smart). And of course I always find myself wondering what he "would have thought about that." I have been left with this image in my mind that my dad was absolutely perfect, because it is easier to gloss over all the flaws and forget about them. My dad is probably the happiest, nicest, and most persevering person I know, despite challenges that are unthinkable to most of us.

Notice that I have that in the present tense—he *is* the happiest, nicest, and most persevering person I *know*. That's right, I didn't used to know him; I know him *now*, because while he may be gone from this earth, he is still very much around. His spirit is very much around. To his dying breath, he left this earth not defined by his ALS but by the traits that made him a model of perseverance I carry with me every day. But indeed, it would be quite some time before I came to this realization.

Chapter Six

I often wonder how I want to die. Of course there's the possibility of living until a hundred and then suddenly dying in your sleep one day simply from old age. There's the quick and sudden death of a car crash or a heart attack where you die before you feel anything. There's cancer, where there is sometimes hope for a cure and going into remission for years before finally succumbing to the effects of the disease after a long and hard battle. There are diseases like Alzheimer's where you survive years after diagnosis, but you aren't really "there" because you are not you; you cannot remember your children let alone your own name. Then there are diseases like ALS in which your mind is perfectly alert but your body is taken away from you. There is no good way to die. But one thing is for sure: ALS is one of the cruelest diseases that can strike a human being. You are sentenced to a life imprisoned in your own body, knowing you are going to die in the next few years.

But at least with ALS, we had time to say goodbye. Every day thousands of daughters around the world lose their fathers to sudden heart attacks, to car crashes, to accidents at work, to death in the line of duty. These daughters had no idea their dad wouldn't be there when they woke up the next morning, no idea their life would be changed from that instant onward. And what if a girl's last thought about her dad was that he was annoying and the last thing she told him was, "I hate you?"

That is something I might have said the day I found out my dad was sick. If he had died that day, July 11th 2012, I would have held that feeling with me for the rest of my life. I would be living with regret, a pit in my stomach, something that I could never make right. But he didn't die that day.

Even though we only had sixteen months together after the diagnosis, short in terms of ALS, and even though we knew he was never going to get better, we had time. We had time to say, "I love you," every night before bed, time to create memories, time to laugh and play cards, time to take pictures, and of course, time for my mom to learn how to do the taxes. We had time to live with no regrets. And even though my dad died suddenly that night in October, we had said everything we had wanted to say. Almost. Of course I would have wanted to say, "I love you," one more time and apologize for every time I had been unkind to him. Of course I would have wanted to hug him one more time, to sit with him and feel him rub my leg like he always did.

In the end, though, as much as it hurt, as many tears that I have shed because his death was "unexpected," it could have been worse. As my friend Emma always used to say after he was diagnosed, he could be hit by a bus and died instantly, without warning, at any time. The same goes for everyone: you simply do not know what the next day will bring, so live each day as if it were your last. I know it's a cliché, but people say it for a reason. From the day we got back from spring break, I began living each day not only as if it was my last day on Earth, but as if it were my last day with my dad.

* * * * *

Sunday, June 16th, 2013- Father's Day

Every year since I was old enough to swing a golf club, the only thing my dad wanted to do on Father's day was to play golf with his family. He didn't want any gifts or a fancy dinner — he just wanted to play golf and have family time. And every year, no matter what kind of mood I was in when

I woke up, I would resist, and Kathryn, once she got old enough, would join in on the temper tantrum. I would insist that it wasn't fun and that I didn't feel like going outside and that I had better things to be doing.

To be fair, golf can be a fairly boring sport. In fact, since you can still play golf when you are a hundred years old or when you incredibly out of shape, I don't even label it as a sport but rather a hobby or a pastime. And it's true; my dad had a real passion for golf, and he would be out on the course at 6 a.m. some days. Maybe the reason he liked it so much is because you can play golf at any age, from two years old until a hundred years old, and no matter how out of shape you are, you can always pick up a club and take a swing. As my mom would say, "golf is a life skill; you can play golf your entire life." Except when you have ALS.

The first time my dad knew something was wrong was when, no surprise, his golf swing felt off and he had gained ten strokes on his game. Just as Lou Gehrig's batting average went down by the day, so did my dad's golf score. My dad was a man of consistency; it was important for him to hit the ball the same way every time and get around the same score (or better) every round he played. So when he started coming home on Tuesday nights frustrated and upset after he played, I was taken by surprise. One day he came home and my mom asked how it went and he simply replied, "Terrible." Not many things were terrible to my dad. But I guess his golf game was that night.

Upon receiving his diagnosis of ALS, he gradually played golf less and less as his hands got too weak to hold the club, his arms too weak to swing it, and his legs too weak to support him and keep his balance. Tuesday nights turned into a time of sitting in his chair, watching Jeopardy; Saturday mornings were characterized by sleeping in and lying in bed.

As I've said before, no one but my dad knew what it was like for him to lose his ability to control his body and do what he wanted it to do, for him to lose the ability to play his favorite sport. Personally, I know what it is like to be badly injured and unable to do gymnastics, the sport that I love. But every time, I knew I was going to get better. That is one of the things that frustrated me throughout my concussion: I knew I was going to get better, but my dad wasn't; he was only going to get worse.

However, not one time did I ever hear him complain. Sure, he would get upset and frustrated, but he never once said, "This is so unfair," or, "Why me?" Maybe he was thinking those things, but he never outwardly expressed them. Yes, it was unfair, and no, we don't know why he was struck. If it were me, I would have blamed the world for such a devastating diagnosis. But my dad never did. And as much as he was hurting inside as he watched his muscles dwindle away, he never complained that he couldn't play golf anymore.

If one day I was told I would never be able to do a flip again, I don't know how well I would handle the situation. I would probably cry and be extremely upset, and then I would go on blaming my parents for something that they had no control over, and then I would blame my coaches, and then I would finally blame my doctor for giving me such a prognosis. Taking away my ability to do gymnastics would be taking away a part of who I am. By robbing him of his ability to play golf, ALS had taken away a part of my dad.

So on Father's Day, 2013, one year after he was diagnosed with ALS, I was determined to do what he had always wanted to do: play golf with his family. At this point he walked like a hunchback, could barely hold onto a coffee mug, and would be knocked over if someone gently bumped into him by accident. But nevertheless, I was determined to get him to swing a golf club. It would not be a family affair without him involved.

This was the first year my dad didn't ask to play golf on Father's Day. So instead, I did. He hadn't been able to play in months, but I nevertheless told him we were going; I didn't tell him he was going to swing a club too.

We live on a golf course, so we literally walked (well, rode in the golf cart) across the street to the driving range. I was going to get my dad to hit a ball. We helped him hobble up to the top of the small hill where you hit the balls, but by the time we got there he was exhausted. Kathryn and I took out our clubs and began driving the balls. I hadn't played in over a year, but somehow, on this day, I was able to hit the ball farther than I ever had before. There is something so satisfying about the "ping" as the club strikes the ball just right, sending it flying across the golf course and out of sight.

My dad was impressed. As he was giving us corrections and advice, he started tearing up. Whether the tears were instigated because he was proud of us or because he was resentful that he couldn't get up and swing a club himself and help us that way, I'll never know. It was probably a combination of both. But that is when I told him to get up. I told him he was going to swing a golf club.

He insisted that he couldn't hold a club anymore, let alone even balance enough to swing it, but I insisted that he would. I was going to help him. I put his golf glove on his left hand and brought out some tape to gently tape his delicate fingers to the club. I walked him over, put a ball on the tee, and told him he was going to swing the club. It didn't matter that he could no longer do it by himself, because I would be right there with him to help him do what he always loved to do.

I stood behind him, supporting his waist with my own body, and grabbed onto his hands. Then I helped him swing the club back and forward. And he struck the ball. On his first try. There was no "swing and miss" as I had expected; he hit the ball dead on. And it went flying. Maybe it didn't go flying like it used to, and maybe it barely went off the ground, but in that instant, my dad started crying. Sobbing.

"No crying!" I told him. But he couldn't help it. I had helped him do what he had thought was impossible, and the emotions that ALS drew out sure did make the tears flow in such a joyous moment.at ALS in him couldn't help but cry at

As much as I knew there was a chance this Father's Day would be my dad's last, deep inside I truly thought I would have one more. As it turned out, I was wrong. But that didn't matter, because I had been determined not to live with any regrets in the time that I spent with my dad.

* * * * *

July 24th , 2013

A little over a year after my dad received the ALS diagnosis, we rented a house on Cape Cod with my aunt, uncle, and two cousins. My dad had just gotten the feeding tube and he had been having a difficult few weeks, so we didn't even know if we were going to go. But my aunt and uncle insisted that we still come. They were willing to accommodate us with anything we needed. If it had been any other family that we were renting the house with, we probably would not have gone. But my aunt and uncle truly had been the backbone for us throughout my mom's cancer and my dad's ALS, coming up every other month from New Jersey just to help out.

During that week on Cape Cod, my dad spent a lot of the time in the air-conditioned house because it was so humid outside. This is one of the first times I started to notice a change in how he was acting. Instead of reading or messing around on his iPad like he normally would, he spent a lot of time just staring, staring at the wall, a chair, and the floor, just as he had on the beach in Grand Cayman. I have no idea what he was thinking about or why he was doing it. Perhaps because he was always so tired and reading just took so much energy. Or maybe it was because he was just thinking about life, about ALS, and, I like to think, about us. In between thinking sessions, he would retreat to the bedroom on the ground level to go sleep. He probably napped at least twice a day, usually after he "got a can" of that feeding tube stuff, and then come out to think some more. I always felt so bad for him; he wanted to go to the beach, kayak, and walk around town with us. One thing he didn't want though: he didn't want anyone feeling bad for him. But how can you not feel bad for someone whose body will not do what he wants it to?

On the day before we left I told my dad we wanted him to come to the beach, but he and my mom stayed back at the house while my sister and I went out with my aunt, uncle, and cousins. We got to the beach and saw how many handicapped parking spaces were available (yes, my dad had a pass, and it was the greatest thing ever — we got front row parking everywhere). Even beach wheelchairs were available, allowing a person to be wheeled down the short ramp and onto the beach. I texted my mom and said she had to bring him.

Sure enough, two hours later, they pulled up. My uncle went and got him and wheeled him down to our spot on the beach. He looked so funny rolling along, with his white baseball cap bobbing up and down as the giant doughnut-like wheels of the chair flopped their way across the sand. We sat him under the umbrella and he stared at the ocean, a smile emerging across his face. It was like everything was normal — two families on the beach, drinking Pepsi and joking around while running in and out of the water. Maybe my dad had arrived in a wheelchair and maybe he couldn't go in the water, but that was okay. This was, once again, our new normal. And I was okay with that.

While on the beach I also got another pleasant surprise. A few weeks before, I had emailed Chobani yogurt, my dad's and my favorite brand of Greek yogurt, and told them how my dad had ALS and one of the few things that he could still eat was Chobani due to its perfect consistency that allowed him to swallow without having to chew. I told them how it was the best thing for him to eat because it perfectly balanced fat, carbs, and protein, not to mention the fact that it's delicious. I emailed them because I just wanted to thank them for everything they do and for making such a great product. So while sitting under the umbrella next to my dad, I checked my phone and saw an email from a woman who worked at Chobani. She was incredibly touched by our story and offered to send us free yogurt whenever we wanted. But what was even more incredible was her genuine concern for us. This was a complete stranger who worked at a large company and probably had a hundred things she needed to be doing. But instead, she took the time to reach out to a family that was going through very difficult times.

Life is all about appreciating the little things: a stranger taking the time to craft heartwarming emails and send free yogurt (time after time, I might mention), a waiter clearing a section so my dad could get to the table more easily, a person offering to help us wheel my dad around.

However, I always wanted to be the only person wheeling my dad around. It was something I could always do that would help him, that would protect him. As we were leaving the beach that day, my dad sitting comfortably in that wheelchair with giant doughnut shaped wheels, my cousin offered to take control and wheel him to the car, but I insisted on doing it. So I was pushing up over the bumps in the sand when I reached the small hill that had a ramp that led to the parking lot. I gave him a nice big shove and the wheels landed on the rim of the ramp, and as I kept pushing, he somehow started to tip backwards. Of course it was my fault, but I like to blame this unfortunate event on the deflated and oversized wheels that were, using my dad's favorite phrase, poorly designed.

As he was tipping over, I remember starting to panic a bit. He was so fragile and I didn't want to be the one that hurt him. I stuck my leg out and the chair smoothly hit and balanced on my foot, my dad's head resting softly above it. I just looked at him and started laughing. And I couldn't stop laughing. He was fine, just in an awkward position. It sure could have been a lot worse, but here I had my dad's head resting on my foot and his scrawny little legs dangling in the air, and I was laughing.

I was laughing because sometimes laughing is the best thing you can do. Sometimes it is the only thing you can do. If I had freaked out, then my dad would have freaked out and in turn so would've everyone around us. My mom doesn't like it when I use that term, "freak out," but that's exactly what would have happened. Laughing made light of the situation and distracted us from the fact that my dad was in a wheelchair in the first place. But most of all, it made the situation memorable and it made my dad laugh too. That is all I could have ever wanted. Instead of coming away truly terrified that his daughter was really going to drive him off a cliff some day, it became the running joke that I was the worst possible wheelchair driver and that I really would someday crash him. If and when the time did come that I crashed him (which I can proudly say did not happen), that would be something to worry about then, but at that moment, it made my dad smile. And that is all I could have wanted.

* * * * *

September 2nd, 2013.

Sitting in my room going through old pictures, I remembered how, one year before, I had been in Paris on the Pont des Arts bridge with my dad. I had told him I wanted to go to see this bridge but I didn't exactly tell him why. When we got there, even I had no idea of its caliber: padlocks of every size, shape, and color lined the fenced edges of the bridge, to the point where it looked more like a solid wall of art, decorated by these glowing locks, than a bridge right in the heart of Paris.

The locks amazed my dad. I told him the story of how people from all around the world come to this bridge and leave their locks to symbolize their eternal love. We started walking to the other side of the bridge and then I stopped. I told him I had a surprise. I reached into my bag and pulled out the two locks. On the way to the airport, my parents' friend Jan had called and told me the story of these locks, and given my knowledge that my dad was sick, I had known I couldn't pass on this idea. In the airport I had sneaked away to *Hudson News* and gotten the highest quality locks I could find — two black and grey plastic ones for an extravagant price of $12.99. One was for my dad and me, the other one for my dad and my mom, signifying their trip to Paris from the year before.

I remember pulling out the locks on the bridge, starting to explain them to my dad, and watching him start to cry. Sobbing. Maybe my dad had cried because of the effects that ALS had on his emotions, because he was sick and was going to die soon and that was not supposed to be the plan. And then I had started crying. I don't really know why; maybe it was because I had finally realized how much I loved my dad and how much he loved me; maybe it was because I couldn't imagine losing him and how I didn't know how I could live without him; maybe it was because he was crying too.

They weren't tears of sadness; they were tears of happiness, happiness that I had been with my dad right there, sharing that moment with him. I pulled him into my arms and squeezed him as hard as I could. I had never been one to connect emotionally with my dad before. That is, until that day.

We found one of the few blank spots in the edge to lock the locks onto, securing them onto the thin metal wire. My dad then asked if we were supposed to throw the keys in the water. I had not even thought about that, but I remember I started tearing up again when he said that. It was a great idea, and I would have never thought of it myself. It was yet another instance of how smart I knew my dad was. So we each threw our key over the side. I will forever have the image engrained in my mind of our keys crossing paths — mine to the right, his to the left, and them dropping into the water at the same time, never to be seen again. And the locks will be there, chained to the side of the bridge, forever. We took a picture. That's the picture that I look at every day when I wake up.

I knew my dad would most likely never see those locks again. I think that was the hardest part of it all for me, one of the reasons I had cried so much. My dad would probably never set foot in Paris again. But I would. I would always come back, and I could always go to those locks and remember the amazing and unforgettable trip to Paris I had with my dad when I was fifteen.

Up until this point, other than the one time watching that oh-so-emotional movie, I had never really seen my dad cry before. But I was really happy he did. It solidified that special moment that we shared, both of us crying on that bridge while people were just kind of looking at us strangely. Not many dads would have started tearing up like he did, and yes, the effects of ALS were probably a factor, but he was crying because he loved me so much, as he always said so incredibly clearly.

The problem was, that day on the bridge, and from that point on, I loved him even more. My mom always says that she loves me more than I will ever know, and it's true, because a mother's love for her child is something that I will not experience until I have children of my own. But dads are different. My dad loved me with all his heart, and he would always tell that to me too. But the hug I gave him on the bridge was an incredible wake up call for me. It was the kind of hug where the love was shared so deeply that my heart started melting. I can still smell his shirt as my nose was pressed on his shoulder, my tears dripping down my cheek, and I can still feel the tight grip of his arms on my back. It was the hug that never ended, the love that never stopped coming.

Nothing would take away the fact that he was sick, but from that day on, it suddenly didn't matter to me as much. The only thing that seemed to matter was the fact that I had time to spend with my dad. Nothing would be able to make up for the time that we were inevitably going to lose, but I had told myself I was going to somehow make the most of it. I loved him too much to waste any of the precious time I had left with him. And although the sadness and anger sure did come, even throughout the hardest times for me during that following winter, the love that I felt that day never once diminished; it only grew exponentially.

The whole trip I kept a journal detailing our adventures and my thoughts written in the form of letters to my dad, and that Christmas I gave him the journal. That day in Paris, the day that I had coined as "the best day of my life," I ended with one single phrase, a phrase that will stay true for the rest of my life: *James Gregory Caldwell is my hero.*

This was one year ago. A lot happened in that year. One year ago he could climb the Eiffel Tower, drink wine, eat crêpes, and walk the streets of Paris, blabbering on about the history of something that intrigued only him. Now he could barely walk, could not eat food, often choked when he drank water, and struggled to speak a few words without being out of breath.

On September 2nd, 2013 it was the one year anniversary of the "best day ever." I honestly had almost forgotten about it with the rush of getting ready to go back to school after summer break, but that afternoon I looked at my phone and saw that it was indeed September 2nd. I had vowed this day to be a holiday and I wanted to do something special for my dad.

He probably didn't remember that it was the day, which made it that much more special when I handed him the card wishing him a happy anniversary of the Best Day Ever. I told him I had a card for him because it was September 2nd. In that moment I like to think he knew what I was talking about, but I really couldn't say what he was thinking.

The card had pictures of us with our locks and hearts everywhere and I told him, as I told him every day, that I loved him and that I was always there for him. On the back I put a picture of him standing behind me and helping me hit the ball when I was three years old; next to it was the picture of me helping him golf from Father's Day. Under the pictures I wrote, "Sometimes it's okay if the roles are reversed and I help you." I added a p.s.: "You'd better not be crying." But of course he was sobbing, just as he had one year ago. And then I started to tear up, just as I too had one year ago.

Dads are portrayed as the superheroes of the world, the people who are indestructible and can take anything. For the longest time I didn't think my dad had any feelings. I thought I could say anything I wanted, and yeah, maybe he would get mad, but I couldn't possibly hurt his feelings, right?

Let's rewind for a second. My dad always used to tell stories of "back when I was a boy," and I always wanted to hear the funny ones about when he would get in trouble or do something stupid. I wanted to hear him tell these stories over and over again, like how he tricked his brother into giving him a dime in exchange for a nickel because he said a nickel was worth more because it is bigger. Needless to say, he got in big trouble for that one and ended up having to give the dime back, resulting in him losing the nickel as well. My dad was crushed—that was a whole half hour of babysitting!

He also used to tell stories about his dogs. He grew up with Boxers, which he described as big dogs that drool and bark a lot. He also had Sir Buckingham, a large dog of a breed that I can never remember but whose name is forever engrained in my mind. I can totally see little Jimmy picking out a ridiculous name like that. But Doc, one of the Boxers, was probably my dad's favorite dog. He used to talk about how Doc had two different barks: one bark for when he saw a squirrel or some other small animal and one bark for when he wanted to go outside or come back in. But one day Doc did not come back in. A man knocked on their door and had Doc in his arms, limp and lifeless. Doc had been running around in the street and the man had accidentally hit him. My dad started crying. To him, Doc was the epitome of "man's best friend," and his best friend was gone.

Jimmy, the little boy who was crying when his dog died, was still the same person fifty years later (plus a few wrinkles and white hairs). Jimmy, my dad, still had feelings. Maybe he didn't cry when our beloved neighbor died (my mom sobbed) and maybe he didn't cry when he was smacked in the face with a balance beam when he was helping set up for a gymnastics meet, but that didn't mean he didn't have emotions that would instigate tears with most people.

I never quite knew what my dad was thinking because he never really showed these emotions. I would obviously know when he was proud of me, when he was happy (he smiled), and when I thought he was sad, but the degree of these emotions was a mystery. Was there a difference between him saying, "I love you" when I went to bed every night and after he read a card that I made him? On the surface, no. He meant it every single time he said those words, but as with all things in life, some moments are more special than others. With ALS, these special moments were filtered out by the tears that would start flowing when emotions got high.

Jimmy, the little boy who grew up to be an extraordinary dad, was not unbreakable, as I had thought. I only began to know how he was truly thinking after he was diagnosed with ALS and subject to those outbursts of crying.

So when he read that card, the tears dripping down his face were the ultimate symbol of his love and appreciation. And that made me want to cry too, because his love for me had driven him to tears. It's easy to bottle up emotions and forget about them, but crying means opening up and letting yourself feel something.

Unbreakable means not letting anything affect you. As the popular saying goes, a true man isn't afraid to cry; a true man isn't unbreakable. I had considered not making the card. I was tired and it was late at night. After all, I told myself I could just do it next year, right? But deep inside I knew I might not be able to. I knew my dad might not be here next year. I was living with no regrets. And it was a good thing I decided to make the card when I did; he died exactly one month later.

My dad may not have been unbreakable, but because of that, he is my superhero. All superheroes have archrivals, and in my dad's case, that archrival was ALS. Some archrivals inevitably defeat the superhero, but that doesn't take away his superpowers. ALS may have taken my dad, as it eventually does with all people at this point, but ALS did not strip my dad of any of his superhero qualities. My superhero fought to the end, losing a battle to a disease of which there are currently no survivors.

Superheroes also have sidekicks, and they can keep fighting even when their superhero is gone. My mom, my sister, and I are my dad's sidekicks, and we fought ALS alongside him and continue to fight it even after he is gone. Because if finding a cure means saving the life of even just one superhero in the future, that is one superhero who can still be there for his child, his partner, his friend. That is a father who will be able to see his daughter graduate from high school, get married, and watch as she cares for him in his old age. And that is reason enough to continue fighting this insidious disease.

Chapter Seven

Before we knew it was ALS, my dad was being evaluated for many diseases. His primary care doctor had sent him to a neurologist after an initial neuro exam that showed some abnormalities. Little did my dad know that his subtle yet characteristic symptoms had led this doctor, a specialist by no means, to quietly suspect ALS. My mom later told my dad, before seeing the neurologist, that if it was ALS it was a death sentence. To this day, she still does not know why she blurted that out. She knew very little about the symptoms of ALS; the only thing she really knew was it was deadly.

My mom is the kind of person who always likes to plan for the worst. She brings extra snacks and bottles of water with her wherever she goes, packs blankets in the car during the winter in case, God forbid, our car breaks down on the way to the grocery store, and carries extra toothbrushes in her carry-on bag when we are flying, just in case our luggage gets lost. My mom is always prepared. But there is nothing she could have done, nothing anyone could have done, to prepare to lose her husband and be left alone to raise her daughters.

ALS was truly one of the worst-case scenarios. Lyme disease is treatable with medication. MS is degrading but isn't fatal. And multifocal motor neuropathy progresses very slowly and is treatable. ALS, on the other hand, progresses rapidly and currently has no effective treatment or cure. Not many diseases currently have a death rate of one hundred percent, but ALS does.

Around August, a little over a year after my dad was diagnosed, I decided I wanted to go to my dad's appointment at the ALS clinic in Massachusetts. My parents were skeptical as they didn't want me to be there if bad news was delivered, the precise reason why I have never been to one of my mom's appointments with her oncologist. But when I make up my mind, the decision has already been made. I knew my parents were being completely honest with us, but I wanted to sit with my dad's doctor and his team of specialists and hear what they had to say.

And so we sat through two hours of respiratory therapists, speech therapists, physical therapists, and nutritionists. I guess this is what happens in ALS clinics. They came with small tips here and there, such as wearing the BiPap more often to help his breathing, wearing a neck brace to decrease the strain, and increasing the amount of nutrition he received through the feeding tube, all suggestions that were pretty much common sense. And while these suggestions would make my dad temporarily more comfortable, they would further limit his independence.

When the physical therapist told him he shouldn't be driving anymore, I knew he wouldn't want to abide by that request. As he would tell me, there were a lot of things he couldn't do anymore, but he could still drive his kids around. Some part of our normal routine could still be conserved, at least for the time being. My dad would be the first one to say if he felt that he did not have complete control at the wheel—he would never do anything to put his kids or anyone else in danger—but until that time came, he would continue to drive. He would continue to have his independence.

The doctor was the last person to come into the room. He spoke very directly with us, going over my dad's symptoms and latest progression. My sister had decided to come too, and we just sat there in our little chairs, looking at my dad as he rested his arms on his cane and exhaustingly took a quick gulp of air in between each word he spoke. The doctor tested his strength on all parts of his body, and with every test, he seemed to remark, "Yep, that's worse." Well of course it was worse. It had been three months since my dad's last appointment, and we had watched him grow weaker every day. So yes, thanks for the confirmation that my dad had in fact gotten worse. How great it felt that all those fancy tests picked up on what we already knew.

I know it wasn't the doctor's fault that my dad was sick, but when there is no explanation for why someone you love is sick, blaming the doctor is only natural. With a sickness like ALS, there is no drunk driver to blame, no cigarettes to link causation; there is only the doctor to blame, the "bad guy" who is the deliverer of this dreadful news day after day.

Soon after, Kathryn and I were ushered out of the room so my parents could discuss "sensitive topics" with the doctor while his nurse rushed back to her office to bring us candy, as if that would somehow make the situation any better. No matter what they were talking about, no matter how bad the news was, I thought it could not possibly be any worse than what I was feeling, sitting there in the waiting room: desperation, anger, resentment. I dug my nails into the leather on the side of the bench, creating a small tear that I kept scratching at. I had come all this way to hear the doctor's honest assessment of my dad, and now I was being kicked out of the room because apparently I wasn't mature enough to handle this "sensitive" information.

I knew what they were talking about. My dad had to make a decision about whether he wanted to be put on a tracheostomy in the near future, a device that would breathe for him. It would also submit him to 24/7 care. I knew he didn't want to live like that, and I knew he had already made a decision. If I were in his situation, I would probably have said the same thing. I have often told my mom that if something ever happened to me, I do not want to be hooked up to a ventilator and left to be a vegetable, taking up space in a hospital room.

But the thing is, with ALS the brain is completely active, so being on a ventilator is not the same thing as someone who is in a coma from a car accident. With ALS, you can still experience the joys of life and watch your kids grow up, but you're often restricted to the confines of your bedroom. Only later did my mom and I realize the technology that has emerged is allowing ALS patients to carry around a portable ventilator that attaches to their wheelchair, allowing them to experience the outside world.

Regardless, my dad made it clear he did not want to be hooked up to a machine. If I were him I believe I would have made the same decision. But sitting in that waiting room, feeling helpless, I could not help but selfishly wish that he would let them "trache" him when the time came. If there was anything that could be done, I wanted those extraordinary measures to be taken. I wanted to be able to go home every single day and tell my dad all the boring details of my day, to engage in frivolous conversation just to take up space. I couldn't help but want to break into that room and tell my dad to change his mind.

Instead I just sat there, digging my nails even deeper into the bench. I also knew the second thing they would be talking about: how much longer he had to live. They do this thing with ALS patients called the forced vital capacity test, and it measures how much air you can force out after taking in a deep breath. Ultimately, it measures how well your diaphragm is working, one of the most concerning aspects in ALS patients. After all, you can live without the ability to move your legs, but once your diaphragm can't work anymore, you can't breathe. In March, just four months earlier, he had measured at fifty-five percent. This means for every breath that you or I take in, my dad only got roughly half of the oxygen that we get and expelled roughly half the CO_2 that we do. You can think of it as breathing through a straw or breathing with a plastic bag over your head — no matter how many times you inhale, you just don't get a satisfactory breath.

In June, he measured forty-five percent, an extremely concerning decrease in a mere three months. A few weeks later when he went in to see if he was a candidate for a diaphragmatic implant that would act like a pacemaker to regulate his breathing, the results were stunning: thirty-eight percent. His diaphragm was functioning nearly one-third of what it was supposed to, a number too low to consider him for the implant.

Now breathe through a plastic straw while a plastic bag covers your head. And then imagine running up the stairs ten times with that hundred-pound weight strapped to your chest. Doesn't sound pleasant? Well, that's the energy it now took my dad to breathe while walking across the room.

I knew that day in the office they were not going to test his forced vital capacity; it was already on a downward trend. They knew it was going to be bad, but they didn't test it. And I'm glad they didn't; we didn't need even more confirmation that he was indeed getting worse, declining faster than we had ever thought.

Remember, this was the doctor who told my dad he probably had five to seven years to live. No wonder I felt anger toward him — he had given me at least five years to enjoy with my dad, for him to see me graduate high school and go off to college, and one year later, I didn't even have to be in the room in that instance to know the number he was giving my dad was far less than four years. Just by looking at him, anyone would know he didn't have anywhere close to that. At the same time, it didn't matter who the doctor was or how friendly he was. My dad had been on a slow progression, and it is still unknown why some people all of a sudden deteriorate more rapidly while others stay on the slow track and can live for years.

In the middle of my rage and fingernail-digging into the bench, the nurse came out to bring us back into the room. I tried to read my parents' faces. Nothing. I'm usually pretty good at it, especially with my mom, but she did not even give a hint. The doctor asked us if we had any questions. Well, of course I had questions—How long did my dad have to live? Why had the disease progressed so quickly? Why was this happening to him in the first place?—but I didn't say anything.

The doctor soon dismissed us as he moved on to his next patient, another person who would once again be the receiver of bad news. I could never be an ALS doctor. They inevitably become the "bad guy," the one a sixteen-year-old daughter blames for her dad's fast decline. They are the doctors who rarely have good news to deliver, only news that tears families apart and causes people to rush to a lawyer to "get their affairs in order." They are the doctors who have to tell people they are never going to get better. There are not going to be any success stories of people who go into remission for years as cancer patients do. At this point in time, there is simply no hope for someone in the end stages of ALS. We knew my dad was not going to get any better.

What frustrated my dad the most was not that he had this disease. After all, people get sick; illness is a part of life. What frustrated him most was that there was no cure for

ALS. The only thing that could be done was to manage the symptoms. If there was one thing I could do to help him, it would be somehow, to help find a cure for ALS. As a teenage girl who hadn't even graduated from high school yet, it was unlikely that I could walk into a lab and devise a plan to develop a drug or treatment that would save my dad. I thought I was powerless in this situation.

I think that's one of the most common thoughts kids have in their life: a young girl cannot make a difference in the whole scheme of things. Maybe recycling one single bottle will not stop global warming, just as one dollar will not cure ALS, but when hundreds, even thousands, of people get involved, that single recycled bottle can turn into colossal amounts of plastic waste that do not end up in landfills; that one dollar for ALS can turn into millions. And those millions of dollars are what are going to cure ALS.

I wanted to do something to help him and all others suffering from ALS. I didn't care if my efforts had virtually no influence on the development of a treatment for ALS; I wanted to do *something*, anything, not to feel so powerless.

The rate at which my dad was weakening was, quite honestly, frightening. The people closest to us knew he was sick, but many people who didn't see him on a regular basis didn't even know anything was wrong. The local ALS Walk was coming up in September, 2013, and my mom and I saw it as an opportunity to help my dad in his fight against ALS. We wanted to create a team for my dad that would walk and raise money in honor of him. We wanted to give the entire community a chance to support my dad. But if I wanted to actually make this work, I needed to tell the community that my dad was sick.

Telling my friends was for *me*. It was me being honest with them about what was going on in my life, and it was me leaning on my friends for love and support. I told the people who needed to know — those I was closest with — but I didn't go around openly offering up this information. And whenever I did tell someone, the tears came every time. Maybe they got less and less with every time I told someone, but they were still there. If I wanted to gather the community together for my dad, I needed to go the un-emotional path in telling them, the exact track I had worked so hard to stay away from.

So in a single afternoon while hyped up on extra coffee for the day, I created a Facebook event page for the ALS Walk and sent out a message to hundreds of people acknowledging that although this was not an ideal way to break the news, my dad had the disease ALS and I needed their help in making this Walk a success. I knew I would get the typical, "Oh my gosh I'm so sorry I had no idea," responses, yet, no matter how similar they all sounded, every single one that I got made me feel, surprisingly, a bit more comforted. It was the support from people I had never really talked to before that made all the difference. My mom emailed hundreds of people information about the Walk as well, and all night I watched the "attending" list grow exponentially. People were sharing the event on their own Facebook pages, and my mom's emails were being forwarded to people we didn't even know. As my mom read the list of people thus far signed up for the Walk, the tears just started flowing down my dad's face. And the tears kept coming, just as the donations and signups did.

We wanted our team to represent the persevering spirit of my dad. He always told me that even as he got weaker and weaker, he wouldn't stop doing anything until he absolutely couldn't do it anymore. No matter how hard it was for him to do it, and no matter how annoying it would be for us that he wouldn't ask for help, he still walked up the stairs and did his dishes, just because he could. Eventually these tasks became virtually impossible for him and modifications needed to be made, but nevertheless, he maintained his attitude; he continued to persevere.

In creating a name for our team we also wanted to incorporate his favorite color, red, which is also the color of his college, Cornell. Red also happens to be the official color of the Walk to Defeat ALS. And with that, Team Red Trekkers was born. Of course there was the red, and 'trekkers' was a testament to his motto in life to keep persevering, to "just keep trekking." And we, of course, were a team, because my dad was all about collaboration, and ALS was not going to be cured by just one person. It was about working together, our team and many others.

Soon after, I contacted the service learning coordinator at the high school. I told her about the event and asked her if the Service Club at the school could make a post about it on their Facebook page. Holly is one of those people I cannot even begin to describe because she is that caring, loving, and selfless. I didn't know her very well at the time, but she responded with one of the most eloquently written emails I have ever read, giving us her love and commitment to making the Walk a success.

I went to the high school right before classes began for the year to hang up posters advertising the Walk, as I had done in businesses all over town. I walked into the lobby and came across a giant hand-painted sign that said, "Walk to Defeat ALS—Team Red Trekkers. Come support the Caldwell Family." I remember staring at the sign for a few seconds before things started to register in my brain. My eyes began to well up in a moment of pure joy.

I ran to Holly's office. I was still in a slight state of shock. I had no idea where the sign had come from or who had made it. As it turned out, the leaders of the Service Club had come in to make a sign everyone would see when then walked into school on the first day. The sign had the potential to overwhelm me, and maybe it did a little. After all, it would mean that *everyone* at the high school would know my dad was sick; it meant all this attention would be drawn to me, attention that I was not sure I wanted. And there was no taking any of this back, no "undo" button that would somehow take away my label as "the girl with the sick dad." But as I looked up at the sign, there was something comforting about it. There's something to be said about people who do something for others out of pure selflessness. People I didn't even know that well had taken time out of their summer to make a sign in support of my family. Maybe I wouldn't be the girl with "the sick dad," because there would be no such label given. Maybe everyone would just see me as normal, because I was making it normal—I was making it okay—to tell everyone you have a sick parent.

As soon as Holly saw me she opened her arms up and offered me a hug, telling me, "You are so loved." I will always remember those words. This woman, whom I didn't even think knew who I was, promised me she would do anything to help me, anything to make this Walk a success. She had already printed out copies of the poster I had made and hung them around the school. Once again, I started crying. I felt like my dad with the constant flow of tears. I took a picture of the sign as I walked out, and I showed it to my dad as soon as I got home. As expected, the waterworks started as soon as he saw it.

With the hanging of the sign at the school, the community was sent over the proverbial edge. Kids put two and two together and realized it was my dad who was sick. In a very short period of time, within three days of returning to school, the word got out to high school and middle school students and the groundswell of people really exploded. I truly wasn't the girl who had the sick dad; I was the girl who was rallying around her dad, doing something no one had ever done before and making it okay to tell the world her dad was sick. Not only this, I was making it okay to ask the community for help.

As the word was spread, more people realized what was happening and how far my dad had declined. People within the community and parents of friends came to the realization that the Caldwell family, with two young girls, was in trouble. They saw the glimpse of sorrow on our faces as our dad was in for the fight of his life. We saw the explosion in the students' and parents' responses and people signing up for the Walk, and it was a realization that there were so many more concerned people out there than we had thought. The event was becoming more than a list of people who said they were going to be there; it was becoming real.

It seemed as though once one person stood up and got involved, another person stood up. And it wasn't just kids anymore; entire families were getting involved. Kids were inspired to come to the Walk, and in turn, so were their parents. People felt compelled to come. All someone had to say was, "Sarah's dad," or, "Kathryn's dad," and parents jumped at that and came.

The week before the Walk was hot and muggy, which made it harder for my dad to breathe. He began to spend the majority of his time sitting upstairs in his chair or in his bed with his BiPap on. A few days before the Walk, my mom looked my dad straight in the eye and told him, "There's no way you're not going to go." He nodded. She once again read him the list of people who had already said they were going, and once again, he started to cry. No matter how exhausted he was, he said he was going to go.

The day before the Walk, family from New Jersey came up to celebrate my dad and to support us at the Walk. We had a T-shirt and sign making party and my friend Grace and former babysitter, ("older sister") Rachel, came over to help us. It was a high-energy evening as we rallied our team spirit among family and friends. Watching my dad with the big smile on his face and his shirt that said "I am Team Red Trekkers" was a reminder of why we were doing this for him. We wanted to make him happy. The evening was just plain fun, with Grace and me searching to try to find our inner creativeness to churn out sign after sign to spread the joy (and red) of Team Red Trekkers.

I couldn't sleep that night. My mind was racing. It had been doing that a lot lately. I was hyped up from all the coffee I had drunk that night in the excitement of the Red Trekkers festivities. I didn't know what to expect the next day or how I would feel. People had been registering for the Walk and we already had thousands of dollars donated to our team. I was thinking about my dad and how bad his breathing was getting. I didn't know if he would be able to make it through the morning at the Walk. Somehow I managed to drift into a semi-restful state of sleep, only to be woken bright and early by the sound of the lawnmowers on the golf course outside our house on a Saturday morning.

And with that, the day began. Buzzed up on caffeine again, I began running around the house collecting all the signs and tables we needed for our setup at the Walk. Kathryn, myself, and my aunt and uncle were the first batch of people to head out, with other family members following behind us shortly. My mom and dad would be one of the final arrivals.

My dad had always been an early riser, insisting he couldn't sleep past 7 a.m. no matter how tired he was, but ALS has its ways of messing with your once-normal life. My dad's new normal was usually still waking up at seven, but then sitting in bed for a few hours before he rallied his strength to get up and go downstairs for the day. Mornings were slow for him, and the day of the Walk, my dad was mustering all his strength just to get dressed and out of the house by 8 a.m. He saw me running around full of energy, and, as it was on a daily basis, I couldn't even imagine how he must have felt. He wanted to be running around in the morning with me, making breakfast and reading his newspaper. Even more, he wanted to be getting ready for a Saturday morning golf game, not a Walk for a disease that would eventually kill him.

Nevertheless, we were determined to make this event one of happy memories and joy, not a sad reminder that he was sick. Holly and her daughter, Louisa, had gone to the school first thing in the morning to get the Red Trekkers sign, and they hung it up on the tent that we had set up. We set up tables with red cloths and family pictures on them, and we had a basket full of bracelets that everyone received that said "I Walked to Defeat ALS" and "Jim's Red Trekkers." People started to trickle in and soon, a large group of Red Trekkers had congregated by the tent. Now all we needed was my dad.

And so the Mom Mobile (a.k.a Toyota minivan) began to roll down the hill of the park, carrying the man of the hour. Driving through the park on that glorious sunny day, the sky bright blue and the dew still glistening on the grass, my mom knew they had prepared a little too well for the cold Maine weather with the sweatpants and long sleeve shirt my dad had on.

We helped him take these extra layers off, and then he announced he had to use the bathroom. We walked him to the Porta-Potty and watched as he struggled to get in and out. But even though he had become weak, he refused to give up his independence completely. Going to the restroom alone was one of those things that he refused to accept help with.

When we wheeled him up in his red wheelchair to the tent where everyone had gathered, he of course, started tearing up. The accumulated mass of people in red was stunning. To see us enveloped in the community was incredible. My parents' former co-workers whom they hadn't seen in years, showed up. Distant friends, people we didn't even know very well, showed up. The entire Service Club at Falmouth High School showed up. Kids I had never even seen before showed up. Many people didn't even register—they just showed up. They came wearing red, bearing a smile, and offering a hug, wanting to show their support to our family and for our family during these trying times. They showed up because they knew Sharon, they knew Sarah, Kathryn, or Jim. They showed up because they couldn't believe this was happening to us. Little did we know it would be a very few short weeks later before they would have to show up again.

As people still gathered, the flurry of activity grew. We were all high on adrenaline, rushing around and greeting people. It was a reunion for my parents, a reunion because the summer was over and we were seeing people from the community and business associates, a living funeral of sorts in that my dad got to see all these long lost faces that would later present themselves at his funeral and visitation the following month. Only this time, he got to look back at their smiling faces. He found the energy to say a few words to each person that came up to see him, and he sure was smiling back at them.

We had people lining up to push my dad in his red wheelchair. With the lull of the summer, many people hadn't seen him in a few months; the progression from June to September was stunning. People walked away that day in shock and disbelief.

We felt what it was like to be in a collective embrace, surrounded by love from the community. Everyone seemed to be there that day. Regardless of what would happen, we knew people were sending as much positive energy, care, and thoughtfulness as possible. Seeing the bright faces of all the kids and students was a reminder that maybe, someday, one of them would help find the cure for ALS or some other disease. But on that day, their smiles were a temporary cure for the sadness of the inevitable effects of this disease. They were a cure for my dad's suffering as he saw how many people stood by him in his fight against ALS.

Every few minutes my dad would tear up from the love of everyone. "You did good, Sarah," he told me as he grabbed my arm while we were walking. "You did good." Those three words made me tear up. In between the sharp, shallow breaths he took, in between the bouts of pain he felt, he found the energy to continue to smile. I had helped make my dad's day a bit better. I had given him even more reason to continue fighting ALS. I had made him smile. And even though he was exhausted, that smile remained on his face for the rest of the week. ALS may have started to defeat my dad's body, but it sure wasn't going to defeat his spirit. And his infectious spirit was all that mattered anymore.

I honestly don't remember much from that day. I was running back and forth between the front and back of the mile long line in clunky boat shoes trying to greet everyone and thank them for coming (yes, I had massive blisters the next morning). I didn't realize how many people were there until I was running that mile long stretch, all one giant blur of red. I was so grateful so many people had come that I felt compelled to talk to every single one. However, in doing so, I forgot to live in the moment.

Instead of walking by my dad's side the entire time, I was walking alongside other people. That is probably one of my only regrets from the entire day. I know it was important to make these people feel appreciated for coming, especially those who we hadn't talked to in a long time or those who we hadn't really talked to at all, but looking back, I wish I had spent more time just walking by my dad's side. These people were there because they wanted to be, because they wanted to support us, and they knew how appreciative we were.

I guess I just didn't realize how little time I had left with my dad. No one did. But the Walk truly did give people a chance to see him who normally wouldn't have been able to before he passed. No one thought it might be goodbye that day. By the time the tail end of Team Red Trekkers got close to the end of the 5k Walk, most people had already finished. Several people were lagging behind with us, wanting to be with my dad when he finished. And so, with my arms on the back of his red wheelchair and my mom and Kathryn right beside us, we crossed the finish line, a sign in my hand that said, "We Will Win The Battle." My dad added to this moment with an iconic fist-pump (caught on camera!) and of course a magnificent smile. Because that is what we are going to do—we are going to win the battle. In that very moment, the hundreds of people cheering us on and flashes of red everywhere, I knew we were going to make a difference. I remember my hands growing sweaty on the handles of the wheelchair and tears flooding my eyes, masked by my sunglasses. There were so many people who loved us, so many people who were willing to hold those signs right alongside us, because they were there to fight the battle too. They were there to fight for my superhero.

Shortly after we crossed the finish line, everyone congregated around the stage where they would announce the top fundraising teams. Going into the day we were third place, so that is what I expected I would get. I stood behind my dad as the announcer read off the third place team and then the second place team, neither of which were Team Red Trekkers. Then she called the top fundraising team, at $23,000: Team Red Trekkers. My dad exploded crying. I went up to represent the team and came back with a twenty dollar grocery store gift card as our "prize" (which I ultimately misplaced and never found). We had raised the most money, but that didn't even matter. My dad was so proud of us. His smile had turned to tears, many times. We had showed him we were going to find a cure for this disease, maybe not be in the next few years, maybe a lifetime from now, but we were going to find one, and the first step was raising awareness of ALS and getting funding, both things that we accomplished on that festive day. And we had the community's full support, with people standing beside us saying, "Let us walk to defeat ALS. Let us stand next to this man, this family, and walk for him."

When we got home, the first thing my dad said to me was, "Thank you, Sarah." It is that small phrase that still makes me tear up to this day. We all could see how happy my dad was, but as soon as we got home, it was evident the Walk had taken its toll on him. He was overheated and exhausted, and he didn't do much but sleep for the next week. It marked the beginning of his final leg of his journey with ALS. There was a part of him that physically just never recovered from that day.

Before the children came along...

Classic picture of Jimbo in the prime of his twenties. Always a man who knew how to have a good time.

The day Jim and Sharon tied the knot,
April 29th, 1990. Dad's mustache was looking
mighty fine that day.

Mom and Dad trekking along through the Wasatch Mountains of Utah.

The early days

Me with Mom and Dad. June, 1997.

He always knew how to make me laugh.

Dad had a thing for waving his arms in the air—I caught on at an early age.

My classic bowl cut looking as great as ever. Cayman Islands. January, 2001.

Dad teaching me to swing a golf club for one of the first times.

Some happy memories

Christmas always was Dad's favorite holiday. December, 2003.

Dad with his two girls before a father-daughter dance— he got us corsages and everything. This was the only time in my life I ever slow danced with my father.

Deep sea fishing in Amelia Island, Florida. Mom sure had a tough time putting a smile on her face after Dad reeled in a 40 pound shark! April, 2006.

Dad always jumping at a photo opportunity with the arms in the air. Mexico, April 2011.

Chapter Eight
October 2nd, 2013

Gymnastics is hard. I'm not going to lie. Five hour practices, pain in every joint, and the joys of doing something like one hundred-twenty pushups. I often call gymnastics the sport that requires you to do a calculus problem or something else requiring just as much concentration, all while sprinting a mile. Apart, these are two very challenging things, and together, they seem almost impossible. But gymnastics requires that same stamina, all while staying mentally alert and concentrating, literally, on not crashing. Flying through the air on the uneven bars, all it takes is one moment of distraction, one moment of fatigue, for you to fall and get hurt.

Bars is the hardest event in gymnastics because it requires the most strength, flexibility, and mental toughness. It demands the most sweat, the most tears, and, for me, the most frustration. But in the end, it gives the biggest reward: swinging around the bars, soaring through the air, and flying from bar to bar is a high no drug can provide.

Gymnastics has a funny way of consuming you, putting you into a zone unlike any other. You forget all about homework, plans for the week, and any fights you recently had with your parents. On October 2nd, I forgot about my dad, sitting at home and struggling simply to breathe. October 2nd was one of the best days of my life on bars.

I usually go home in between school and gymnastics. I am at the gym for five hours, so I don't like not seeing my parents from 7:30 a.m. to 9:00 p.m.. However, on October 2nd, I chose to participate in a math competition after school, so I went straight to the gym afterward and did not go home.

Before leaving that morning, I knew my dad had had a bad night and would have a bad day. I told him I wanted to stay home from school to spend time with him and help him in any way, giving my mom, who was tirelessly caring for him, a break. He assured me he would be okay and that he was just going to sleep all day. He said my mom would call me right away if she needed anything. I persisted, but in the end gave in.

I kissed him on the top of his sweet little balding white head and smiled. "I won't be home after school today, but I'll see you when I get home. I love you," I told him. I had been fighting off a cold and had tried to avoid contact with him recently, but kissing him goodbye was important.

He sat there, closed his eyes, bobbed his head as he swallowed, and managed to squeak out an, "I love you, too." At this point, talking was exhausting for him. He used the speech generating technology on his iPad, but he hated it because he believed it was once again forcing him to succumb to his disability and admit defeat. Many times he simply nodded or gave a thumbs up or down, but in this moment, he managed to use what little energy he had to tell me he loved me.

He smiled and I headed out the door. Little did I know that would be the last time I would ever see him smile, the last time I would feel the warmth of his little head, the last time I would ever hear him say, "I love you."

It was 7:05 p.m. when I first knew something was wrong. I know it was this time because we were almost finished with bars, and I had wanted to stay a few extra minutes before moving on to the next event. I was having a great practice. But everything changed when my other coach walked into the gym.

She had kind of a funny look on her face as she watched me take my turn. Afterwards, I looked to her for any comments about my routine. She just looked at me. "Sarah, your mom is here. It's okay, you can go," was all she said.

In that instant my life changed forever. I knew something was wrong. I sprinted upstairs to get my clothes and instantly started crying. My mom had never come get me before. Something was wrong with Dad. My coach opened the door to the locker room with tears in her eyes. "I did it. I was sick and I got near him. I did this, I made him worse," I sobbed.

"No, honey. You didn't do anything." But then she started tearing up too. She kissed me on my forehead and walked me downstairs.

I saw my mom and we went outside. Her friend Robin, and our neighbor, Sue, were by the car. Something was very wrong. I nearly shouted at my mom, "What's wrong, what happened?" Her response will always be ingrained in my head and will haunt me for the rest of my life. "Sweetie, Dad didn't make it." Those five words changed me for the rest of my life.

My heart was racing so hard I felt as though it would rip out of my chest. I started feeling dizzy. I could no longer feel the weight of my feet on the ground. My mom hugged me, Robin's hand on my head as she tried to comfort me. I felt pain all over.

Three minutes before, I had been swinging on bars, my hands grinding against the leather of my grips, blood oozing from the blisters, my arms burning from exhaustion. But that had been a good kind of pain. This was a different pain. It was the pain of sorrow, the pain of loss. The pain as the tears flowed out of my eyes and landed on my mom's shoulder. It was the pain of knowing I would go home and my dad would not be there. There would be no feeding tube that night, no call to my mom for water, no shuffling in the middle of the night to go to the bathroom. I knew I would go home to never hearing my dad's voice again or feeling the warmth of his body as I hugged him goodnight.

Robin took my car and drove it home, and my mom and I rode with Sue to go pick up my sister at her friend's house. I sat in the middle of the back seat with my head on my mom's shoulder and the flow of tears came to a halt, at least temporarily. My mom ran me through the events of the day. I wanted to know everything.

4:45 p.m.

My dad was sitting in the chair in his bedroom, his stick thin legs resting on the footstool. He turned to his right and picked up his plastic water cup from the nightstand, his arms shaking as he lifted the rim to his chapped and dry lips. He set the cup down. He sniffled and tried to cough, but he was too weak to clear his lungs. My mom helped him stand up so he could use the bathroom. He walked with his hands on his walker, shuffling his feet along the carpet, his head dipped down at a ninety-degree angle.

He shuffled back. He pushed the walker to the side and plopped down into the chair, his muscles fatigued beyond exhaustion. He sat there for several minutes over labored breathing. He reached over to the nightstand again and grabbed his iPad. His hand shook as he swiped the unlock button. Into his speech-generating app he typed, "CO_2 buildup."

That was what the hospice nurse had told them the day before. She said he wasn't getting good air exchange, and the carbon dioxide from the air and from his cells was building up in his lungs; his diaphragm and chest muscles were not strong enough to exhale all the way. That was what was causing his sleepiness.

My mom looked at him and saw the sorrow in his eyes. She asked him if he wanted her to call the doctor. He just shrugged. There was nothing they could do. She didn't know how to make him more comfortable, to help him in any way. But he looked okay, better than he had that morning. It was his cold that was making it even more difficult to breathe, his cold that I had brought into the house when I came home sick the week before. His nose and chest were still congested, but he had started to feel a bit better, so much so that he told my mom she could go out and get the cables we needed to hook up the new TV.

He had always told my mom when he wanted her to stay. If he wasn't feeling well, he would tell her. So when he waved his arm and told her she could go, as much as she hated to leave him alone, she knew she would only be gone for an hour or so. And then my dad's friend, Tom, was going to meet her back at the house to help set up the TV.

She kissed him goodbye and said, "I love you." He gave a thumbs up. It was one of the only times he didn't say, "I love you," back. He was too tired. She put his phone on the table and told him to call her if he needed anything. She told him she could rush home at any minute. She said not to get up, that she would be back in an hour. He bobbed his little head and gave a thumbs up again.

It was the best goodbye she could have given. There is nothing else she could have done.

Somewhere around 5:30 p.m.

You know that pain in your chest you get when you hold your breath for a long time? That is not from lack of oxygen; it is from the build up of carbon dioxide. Having no oxygen is not what kills you — it is from the carbon dioxide not being expelled.

My dad was just sitting in his chair, probably staring at the wall. He was breathing in and out, his chest muscles burning with exhaustion, as he tried to force air into his lungs. His nose was still congested and he had to breathe through his mouth, forcing his already weak chest muscles to work harder. He was too weak to exhale hard enough, too. Carbon dioxide had been building up in his lungs for weeks.

At some point he probably realized he had to go to the bathroom again. He pushed himself up from the chair and grabbed onto his walker. He shuffled along the carpet back to the bathroom. At this moment the carbon dioxide levels in his blood had risen too high, making his blood acidic. His body could just no longer compensate. He probably didn't even realize what was happening. His breathing would have increased and he might have started to feel lightheaded. His legs collapsed under him. He fell to the floor and landed on his side. He didn't feel anything. He just went to sleep. His heart stopped beating, and his muscles relaxed. He was finally at peace.

* * * * *

As we pulled up to get Kathryn, I could see her and her friend in the room above the garage, the light flooding through the darkness where we stood in below. They were laughing and smiling. I stopped for a moment. In a few seconds, my sister's world would be turned upside down.

But at least for that moment, life was good for her. She was just a normal kid smiling and goofing off with a friend. After we rang the doorbell, I didn't know when I would see that smile again.

She was at the door within seconds. She knew something was wrong but she didn't know what. She would later tell me she thought Dad had gone to the hospital or something, because if it had been anything worse, Mom would have gotten her sooner.

She grabbed her stuff and we guided her away from the house. "Kathryn," my mom began, "Dad died." I bit my lip.

Kathryn's eyes welled up faster than I thought was even possible. She shrieked in pain. "But, but I didn't get to say goodbye. I didn't say goodbye to him today. I didn't tell him I loved him," she screamed. My sister has always been the crier in the family; I have been the yeller. When we were little she used to make herself cry on purpose so she could get me in trouble. Even as a baby, my mom would say she cried like no baby she had ever seen. It wasn't that she was unhappy; she just liked to cry. It became her way of dealing with any emotions she was experiencing, from anger to frustration to sadness.

So when these tears of sadness and shock and desperation started, there was no stopping her. And I didn't want to. I hugged her as hard as I could. My mom and I echoed in saying that Dad knew she loved him no matter what.

But still, she didn't get to say goodbye that day. Deep down she knew telling him she loved him one more time wouldn't have made a difference, but it's still something she will often think about. In the same way, I know, deep down, that I wasn't to blame for getting my dad sick or causing him to die any faster, but I still carry it with me to this day no matter how many times I am told it wasn't my fault.

My mom, Kathryn, and I squeezed in together in the back seat of Sue's car and began the quiet drive home. I didn't even bother to put my seatbelt on; I wanted to be as close to them as I could. This marked the beginning of our journey together as a team of three, the beginning of car rides without Dad there with us. Mom told us we didn't have to go home if we didn't want to — my dad was still there and so were police officers and many other people — but Kathryn and I both immediately said we just wanted to be home.

I opened the car door as soon as it pulled into the driveway and we rushed inside. A woman (whose name I never registered) introduced herself as a hospice nurse. She had stringy gray hair and was wearing some sort of colorful scrub-type outfit. If I had seen her on the street I would have said she was a bit odd, but in that moment, she was the most comforting person I could have asked for. I told her I was going up to see my dad. That is my personality in a nutshell — always doing what I want and not letting anyone get in my way.

I turned to go upstairs only to run flat into a fairly large police officer blocking the way. My mom was right behind me and said it was okay if I went up. "You need to prepare yourself," the officer said. There was nothing aggressive or heartless about the way he said it, but the very nature of that comment made me want to punch him in the face. Well, of course I needed to prepare myself. My dad was lying dead on the floor of my parent's bathroom. I knew the policeman was just doing his job, but, like my dad's doctor, I just wanted to blame him for what had happened.

Sue had told me my dad wouldn't look like he normally did. The color would be drained from his face and his skin would be cold to the touch. It was just his body; his soul was already in Heaven. I didn't want to believe her until I saw him there on the floor.

His skin was as pale as his white hair, his lips drained of all their color. He didn't look like the person I had left that morning, but he did look peaceful. His eyes were shut and his arms rested on his stomach, folded, as if he were sleeping. I couldn't help but think how blood had flowed through his veins just over an hour before.

I immediately burst out crying. Sue's husband Charlie put his hand on my back as I sobbed into my hands. It felt so weird to break down like that in front of so many people, so many people that I barely knew or had not even met before, but I didn't care. Talk about expressing my emotions. The hospice nurse sat me down and just talked to me. I didn't even really know what she was saying, but whatever it was made me feel a fraction of a bit better. My mom came in and everyone stepped out so we could have alone time with my dad.

I walked up to his body and knelt down. I knew that was how I was supposed to think of it—his body. It wasn't my dad. Yet it *was*. He had the same hair on his head, the same stubble on his face, the same tiny little nose.

The lace on my dress suddenly felt itchy. I told myself I would never wear it again. I felt shaky. I touched his forehead. Ice cold. Not room temperature or slightly cold— ice cold. He looked older and frailer than I would have remembered, his stubble whiter and longer than I would have thought. His white T-shirt seemed too big and his plaid pajama pants too dull. "This isn't Dad," I kept reminding myself over and over again. "Dad has already gone to

Heaven; this is just his body." Only just that morning I had kissed that same head goodbye and felt the warmth as the blood flowed through him. And now it was ice cold.

My mom and I sat there for a few minutes in silence. I just stared at him. I had never seen a dead person before. The tears had stopped—I had reached the point beyond sadness where it was simply too much effort to cry anymore. My mom said an Our Father prayer and then we got up. It felt so weird to just leave him there like that, like we were abandoning him.

I went downstairs and sat on the couch with my mom and Kathryn, Robin and Sue. I ate a cookie that wasn't gluten free, just because I wanted to. Nothing mattered right then. It didn't matter if I would feel sick the next morning. My dad had died, and nothing could hurt as much as that.

The funeral home people came and got my dad, bringing his wrapped body down the stairs on a stretcher. I wanted to watch but they wouldn't let me. And just like that, his body was gone, in the hands of complete strangers. I kept thinking about how he would never be back to our house, the house he and my mom moved into when they came to Maine seventeen years ago. This was the house they had raised their children in and built a life in. And he would never be back.

My mom went into the formal living room to start calling family and close friends to tell them Dad had died. Dad had died. I kept repeating it to myself over and over again. I looked at my phone. 8:35 p.m. Everyone at the gym knew something had happened when I sprinted out just an hour earlier. They would just be getting out of practice. I already had several texts from my friend Emma, whom I was right next to before I ran out: "Are you okay?" "What is happening?" "Call me." I took a deep breath and pressed call.

Every day when I was home with my concussion, Emma would text me about what had happened at gymnastics. She is that person in my life who has me completely figured out and always remembers the weird things, like how I don't like fantasy books or how I prefer small forks to big forks. To quote *Grey's Anatomy*, if I murdered someone, she's the person I'd call to help me drag the corpse across the living room floor. After all, when you spend twenty hours a week with someone, enduring practice after practice and laughing through the unbearable because there is simply nothing else to do, you have no choice but to become best friends with your teammates.

We would have conversations via text that went on for hours, and as I was complaining about my life and how sad I was, she would remind me of how lucky I am. She would remind me that I had come so far in my recovery, that I am smart and talented and have lots of friends and am not awkward in social situations as she is. As I would continue on about how much life sucks, she would often respond in her characteristic sassy and sarcastic yet genuine and kind way. "You're way less screwed up than ninety-nine percent of people on television, so congrats," is one of my all-time favorites. Translation: you've gone through way more than you should have at this point in your life and I know it's not fair, but always remember you've got a lot going for you.

But that night she knew there was no time for joking around. She picked up on the first ring.

"Can you come over? My dad died." That was all I said. Blunt and to the point.

"I'll be right there." She hung up. Ten minutes later Emma and her mom walked in the back door. She threw her arms out and gave me a hug—a hug that seemed to last forever—and we sat down on a bench where I gave my first *shpiel* about how my dad was "in a better place" and looked "so peaceful." Yes, it was true, but it was also my completely fake way of communicating my emotions, once again putting a mask on everything like I know how to do oh-so-well.

My mom came in and we sat there with them for a while just talking. Emma didn't even have to say anything—having a friend there, someone you trust and whom you love, makes everything better, even for just a second. After a while they left, Emma off to do homework. I kept forgetting that life for everyone else was still going on. My life may have temporarily stopped, but the entire world had not been put on pause because my dad had died.

When my mom went back to the living room to call more people, I knew it was time for me to make some calls before anyone else found out through word of mouth instead of directly from me. Telling Emma what had happened was easy because she already knew that something was wrong. With everyone else, I would have the lovely task of telling them out of the blue that my dad had died.

I dialed Grace's number. Grace always asked about my dad and how he was doing, and she was one of the few people I wouldn't give the generic, "He's doing all right," answer. I had texted her the day before and said that he was getting a lot worse after I had given him a cold. I told her how worried I was. But this worry was over the fact that maybe he would have a few restless nights, not that he would die.

"Hi Sarah!" Grace said when she picked up the phone. She sounded cheerful yet busy doing something, probably biology homework. She probably thought I had a question about the project that was due the next day.

"Grace, I have to tell you something." I swallowed. I didn't know how to do it. "My dad died."

While there's no good way to tell someone your dad has died, there's no good way to respond when your friend tells you this. She was shocked. I don't even remember what she said. There was nothing that could be said. She asked if I wanted her to come over. Well, of course I did. There were too many adults around I really didn't feel like talking with. My mom and her friends were on the phone with people, and I had no idea where Kathryn was. I couldn't just sit there and stare at the wall. At the same time, I didn't want to inconvenience Grace. It was already past nine. I told her she didn't have to come, that I was fine.

"No you're not, Sarah," she said. "I'm coming over. I'll be there in a few minutes."

I took a deep breath. Asking for help is hard, but sometimes it's even harder to accept help. I didn't want to admit I needed help in the first place. When she asked if I wanted her to come over, I had wanted nothing else. Of course my first answer was that I was fine, that she didn't need to come all the way over to my house. But I wanted her to anyway. I wanted nothing more than to have someone sitting there with me, to not be alone.

I hung up and dialed Holly's number to tell her before she found out from anyone at the school. She, like everyone else, was shocked. She had seen him at the Walk less than a month ago. Sure, he'd looked weak and was having trouble breathing, but he could still walk and talk and smile. No one knew he had less than a month left.

It was the sense of despair in Holly's voice that let me know I was not in this alone. "You are so loved," she told me. It is what she always tells me. After I hung up I decided I couldn't call anyone else. They would find out from other people and that was just how it was going to be.

Grace showed up at the front doorstep in a matter of a few minutes. She gave me a hug, the kind of hug that made me feel all warm inside. She didn't even say anything. She didn't have to. We grabbed a box of Oreos, once again, just because, and we sat in my bedroom for over an hour and just talked. We cried and smiled and laughed. I was already getting dozens of texts from people that I simply didn't have the energy to respond to. As Grace told me though, no one expected me to respond; they were just letting me know they were there for me. As much as the next few days would be incredibly difficult for me, my closest friends and even some people I didn't know that well were going to have a hard time too. Because what are you supposed to say to someone who just lost her dad? "I'm sorry" doesn't seem to cut it, and people know that, but it's the only thing they know how to say. The truth is, it doesn't matter what anyone says. It matters that the person knows you are there for them. I thought it would be overwhelming getting all these texts, but it was strangely comforting. It was the people I didn't know were out there that reminded me how much this community had our backs.

Grace eventually left and so did all the other people in our house. It was around eleven o'clock and the house was silent. It was just Mom, Kathryn, and me. This was our new normal. This was our new life. We sat on the couch and didn't move. We talked and cried, but most of all, we just sat there with each other. Then around 2 a.m. my sister went off to her room and I crawled into bed with my mom. She slept on my dad's side and I slept on hers. I held her hand and we quietly cried together.

I slept in my dad's Hump Day T-shirt. He'd had a thing for "Hump Day." When my aunt and uncle visited a few months before, we were all watching TV together and a GEICO commercial came on with a camel walking through an office saying "Uh oh. Guess what day it is? HUMP DAYYYY." My dad thought it was the funniest thing ever and we began quoting it all the time. So when my aunt and uncle saw a Hump Day shirt somewhere, they mailed it to us. We had gotten it just a few days before, and my dad hadn't even gotten the chance to wear it. If anything though, the gift made a positive mark on one of his last days here on Earth. It made him smile.

Crazy things happen on Hump Day. They say once you get past Wednesday, the "hump" in the week, getting through Thursday and Friday will be easy and then it is the weekend. Just like the hump on the camel's back, it is the rough patch in the week. I found out my Dad was sick on a Wednesday. That was a hard day. And he died on a Wednesday. That was an even harder day. But the thing about Hump Day is that it's the worst it gets. Those two Hump Days were, thus far, the two worst days of my life. But because it's Hump Day, it gets easier after. It may be a while, but things will get better.

My dad died on Hump Day. The funny thing is though, he got over the hump too. Wherever he went after he died, he had gotten through Hump Day. He had crossed over to the "other side" where life is easier and more peaceful, the so-called Thursday and Friday. He was stuck on a Wednesday for sixteen months as he battled ALS, a constant uphill struggle as he gradually lost control of his body and simple tasks became impossible.

My dad was a big hiker, and he would always tell me the exertion is always worth it when you get to the top. The climb may be exhausting and the altitude may make breathing hard, but once you get there, the view is spectacular. My dad's journey with ALS was undoubtedly an uphill battle all the way. As with any hike, you learn something on the way up. For some people it might be they discover their love (or hate) for hiking, they might become closer with someone, or they may realize the need to get in better shape and bring more bug spray next time.

With his battle with ALS, my dad learned some things about himself too. He had always been the guy who could do anything athletically without much effort, and for the first time, he was unable to do the things he wanted, from hiking a mountain to buttoning his shirt. Because of ALS, he had to learn how to be patient and ask for help, neither of which was easy for him.

Toward the end, he faced a hike through life that proved to be one of steepest possible. But that day, Wednesday, October 2nd 2013, he reached the end. When he reached Heaven or wherever he went, he was able to see the spectacular view. He could play golf again, he could climb mountains again, and he could enjoy drinking his expensive bottles of red wine again. He could watch his beautiful daughters grow up in the world and know that "he did good" in raising us. The hard part was over for him. But it was only the beginning for us.

On the night of October 2nd 2013, I joined the Dead Dad Club. It's a club you never want to join, and until you join the club, you can never truly feel the pain. In the next few days, flowers and cards and casseroles of all different types arrived at our door; people we would have least expected showed up, and the well wishes and gestures of sympathy never stopped coming. But until you see your father lying in a coffin, until you stand for hours at the visitation and accept peoples' sympathies over and over again while trying somehow to plaster a smile on your face and not break down crying, you won't get it.

Everyone handles his or her joining of the Club differently. For me, denial worked pretty well. It wasn't denying that my dad had died—I had obviously seen the lifeless body lying on the floor that night, and I woke up every day after that knowing he wouldn't be coming back. My denial was more along the lines of denying my feelings, per usual.

Of course I cried and of course I was sad, but most of the crying I did was limited to the day he died, the first time I saw him at the funeral home, and then at the funeral itself. Even when I woke up the morning after he died, I wasn't even that sad. I just felt kind of numb.

The day after my dad died I woke up to an email from Ms. Magnuson, my advisor at school and beloved biology teacher. I often would have long discussions with her about life and what was going on with my dad, and she would just talk to me. And it wasn't a one-way street—she talked about herself too. Her mom had died after a horrible battle with cancer, and although she hadn't lost her dad and she was older than I was when her mom first got sick, she understood me. I liked talking to someone other than my social worker, someone who knew what I was going through, yet was still on the "outside" and wouldn't just agree with everything I said. She wasn't afraid to challenge me when I said something ridiculous or tell me I needed to stop bottling up my emotions. She was the one who told me it is okay not to be okay. She was the one who insisted on emailing all my teachers at the beginning of the school year to let them know I may randomly leave class or not finish my work if it meant spending time with my dad or if it had been a hard night.

In that email I opened at six-thirty that morning after a restless night's sleep, she was the person to tell me that there is nothing anyone can say, nothing anyone can do, to make everything okay — because everything was not okay. She reminded me that life is tragic and unfair and there are no reasons why any of this was happening. She reminded me it was okay to cry and to lean on others and ask for help, because I'm supposed to be sad. I'm not supposed to be okay.

But for me, the only way I knew how to proceed, to live in this world without my dad, was to pretend I was okay. I had to continue living life as normal. Life had seemingly been put on pause, and all I wanted was for the play button to be pressed and for it to skip across the funeral. I wanted to go back to school and gymnastics, because I felt okay. I was sad, of course, and I had known this would be coming, maybe just not so suddenly. Regardless, I was in a place where I felt as though I had already done all my grieving. I thought that I had prepared myself, that all my crying had already been done. I told myself I had already done most of my grieving when I found out he was sick.

But that was a different kind of grieving. It was grieving about what the future may bring, grieving about how we would only have a few years left with my dad before he died. Even as he got sicker and sicker, his immanent passing still hadn't become truly real, because what we were all sad about had yet to come. But once he died, once the event of all our worries had become reality, once I had been left without a father, a whole new chapter in our grieving had opened. I refused to accept that fact, pushing aside any emotions, telling myself I had already done all the work of "processing them" and "talking about them." Little did I know it is a very different thing to have a sick father and to have a dead father.

Even when life for us seemed to go on pause after my dad died, it was quite the opposite. Family flew in from all around the country, and friends were constantly stopping by to drop off even more food, so our house was never quiet. I didn't have to go to school or gymnastics, even though I wanted to, because we needed to prepare the "arrangements," i.e. the funeral.

The morning after my dad died, Rachel came over to our house. She took the day off work just to be with us; she was my dad's other "daughter," the big sister I never had. I had forgotten she would be hurting as much as we were. I forgot how much everyone else would be hurting. Jim Caldwell had been my dad, but he had also been a husband, a friend, a son, a brother.

My mom had to go to the funeral home and pick which "package" she wanted, just like the packages you choose from for back to school pictures or for the kind of hotel room you want. In other words, as with any business, what you choose all comes down to how much money you want to spend. Funeral homes are a business, and a relatively successful business too—what widow is going to get anything but the best, the fanciest and most expensive, coffin and service plan available?

My task was to go through old photos to display at the visitation. I spent hour after hour going through old boxes, sorting pictures, and scanning them to my computer. My mom told me to select a few; I selected hundreds. I became obsessive over finding every picture I had ever remembered seeing, of sorting through and finding memories from all facets of my dad's life, but not once did I cry when looking at any of them. In fact, I didn't have any feelings at all. There was nothing I could do to undo the fact that my dad had died less than twenty-four hours before, but somehow, immersing myself in this project, becoming obsessive over everything and trying to be as efficient as possible, gave me a purpose. It gave me a reason to keep going, a reason not to break down crying. It became the means by which I would not have to sit down and talk with someone about how sad I truly was.

I also had to prepare a "speech," as I called it, for the funeral. From the day I found out my dad was sick I had been preparing what I wanted to say. I used to stand in the shower with tears dripping down my face, tears no one else knew existed, and pretend I was standing up there at his funeral. I would go on and on about all the ways he was the most wonderful dad I could have ever asked for and tell stories of the day he taught me how to ride a bike without training wheels and when he broke the news to me at age three that I would have to pee in the woods while on a hike because there wasn't a bathroom.

I practiced over and over again what I wanted to say. But when it came down to actually writing something, my mind was blank. Draft after draft, hour after hour, I kept pressing delete on my computer, because no matter what I said, I would not be doing justice to the amazing person my dad had been.

* * * * *

As I sat next to my mom in the first row pew in the church, Kathryn on her other side, my vision was fixated on my dad's coffin, two feet away, a white cloth draped over it and my mom's crystal cross sitting on top. I couldn't help but imagine what he looked like, lying in there, all cold and pale and alone. For some reason, ever since the day he died, I had been excited for his funeral. Okay, maybe "excited" isn't the right word, but for some strange reason, I was.

Maybe it was because I just wanted to get it over with, or maybe because I knew I would get to see all my friends.

Only when I found myself sitting there, next to my dad's coffin, did I realize I should have been in school taking a math test that day. I wasn't supposed to be at my own father's funeral. It was as if I were living in the body of some other sixteen-year-old girl, because this wasn't what was supposed to be happening. Any feelings of excitement quickly vanished. I turned cold.

The routine of Catholic prayers and music almost felt like just another church service, another hour in which I felt free to daydream and think about all the other things I would rather be doing, the way I always did on a typical Sunday morning. But that day, rather than wishing I could be off with friends, I wished I could be taking that math test, because that's what I should have been doing. I just wanted my dad to come back and for everything to go back to how it had been a week before. Instead, I was at his funeral, about to get up and give a eulogy, and he was lying in a wooden box that wasn't nearly as fancy or elegant as I had imagined.

As much as I didn't want to be there, the whole thing did pass fairly quickly, probably because I was distracted by all the random thoughts flooding my brain. I kept thinking about the math test and about a really great gluten-filled muffin I had had for breakfast. Toward the end, my dad's friend, Dave, went up to tell some funny stories from the past fifteen years and talk about what a wonderful husband, dad, and friend my father was. Then my uncle talked about my dad's wonderful spirit, personality and fun-loving manner that was evident his entire life. Oh, and he also confirmed that he is in fact seven years younger than my dad, so, no, they are not twins as everyone thinks. He had just been blessed with the same wonderful balding headline and wrinkled forehead seven years earlier.

I had a smile on my face as I smoothed my black dress across my legs and stood up to go give my little speech. I shuffled toward the podium, walking toe over heel, as my bright red stilettos sunk into the carpet. Everyone was wearing a "splash of red" as a tribute to my dad's Team Red Trekkers and ALS awareness, brightening the somber black of the funeral attire. I walked up the three steps to the microphone and looked into the swarm of people in the pews. I had never seen the church full like this. Every single seat was filled, the chairs along the edges included, and people were even standing on the sides. As I stood up there, my brain did not register a single face; all I saw was a giant mass of people, all staring up at me with flushed faces and tears in their eyes as I was about to tell my version of the man my dad was.

"Wow there's a lot of you here," I began. Then I started to panic a bit. I had improvised. I wasn't supposed to do that. I couldn't break down crying in front of all these people. I paused. I tried to register who was there in the crowd of people, but I truly couldn't pick out any individuals. I remember feeling the strange pulsing in my abdomen begin to pound against my dress, my heart racing from the adrenaline flooding my body. I waited a few more seconds and then finally spoke.

"Ever since I knew about my dad's diagnosis of ALS, I have been planning on what I would say at his funeral."

People gave a nervous laugh. Were they supposed to laugh at that? It wasn't supposed to be funny. I hadn't planned on them doing that. My heart sped up again. I suddenly felt incredibly awkward standing in front of all these people — every single person in our immediate family, all our closest friends, the superintendent of the school district, my dad's business associates, random people I would have least expected to show up. I looked directly through them as they stared back at me. And as I stood up there, I had the attention of every single person. But in this one-way street, I had no idea who those people actually were. I was blind to their very existence. I took another deep breath. I thought back to all those nights in the shower, practicing for this very moment. And with that, I began my story.

"I could not imagine what it would be like to lose my father. My father, the man who taught me how to tie my shoes, ride a bike, play cards, swing a golf club, and how to rise again when I failed. My father, the man who always had a smile on his face, was going to be taken away from me far too soon. I knew he would not be here for my sister and me as we grew up, and would not grow old with my mother, as they had planned. But in my dad receiving this fatal diagnosis, no matter how horrible it may have been, I was given the gift of time to spend with him and a chance to reflect on the life he created for us. And as I stand here today, the most valuable lesson my dad has left with me is to remember to just 'be happy and nice to others.'

'A few years ago, we were having dinner one night with some people we had never met before. Later that night, a woman came up to me and said, 'You know, your dad is a really great guy.' Now, after two hours of simple banter about innocent subjects, this woman had managed to have a glimpse into the true personality of Jim Caldwell. And honestly, there is no better way to define my dad than a 'great guy.' He is the person who is always smiling and looking for the good in others. He is the person who never gets mad or raises his voice, and goes out of his way to kiss his daughters goodnight every evening. He is the person who always reminded me to just 'be happy' even when I was frustrated with the world. In the last few months of his life when ALS was rapidly taking over his body, he always managed to crack a joke or give a small smile and a thumbs up. He could have easily retreated into a hole of darkness, but my dad chose to rise up and live every day as best that he could. I cannot imagine the strength he must have had to continue living life for what it is despite such an awful diagnosis.

'But nothing frustrated him as much as the fact that there is no cure for ALS. No matter how much he fought, he knew he would not be able to overcome this disease. I was worried it would take its toll on him and strip him of his famous personality, so I made it my mission to do everything I could to keep that smile glowing on his face. The Walk to Defeat ALS last month was a spectacular event that reinforced the community's love for him. And let me tell you, I had not seen my dad have that big of a smile in months.

'No one would have thought he would go so quickly; we thought we had a few more months. But for the last few weeks he had been hanging on by a thread. This insidious disease was finally taking its toll on him, and he was no longer the vibrant person that everyone knew him as. But right now, he is looking down on us, and his smile is as big as ever. He can laugh, talk, play golf, and enjoy the little things in life that he could not these past few months. And as much as we all miss him and wish he were still here with us, we must remember that he will always be with us wherever we go. He will always love us and cherish the wonderful memories we created together. Today, he leaves us with a legacy of strength, determination, positivity, and love. And to all of you, my mother, Sharon, my sister, Kathryn, and I would like to say 'thank you' from the bottom of our hearts and to always remember to 'Just keep trekking.'"

I was done. Tears were visible in nearly everyone's eyes. Except mine. I had remained cold and detached, and while what I had said was full of fervor, it was very much emotionless on my part. My mom then unexpectedly stood up and walked to the front. It wasn't in the plan to have her talk. But I am forever grateful she did.

In front of hundreds of people, hundreds of people who love and support our family, she talked to us. She didn't read off a speech like I did; she truly reached us. I don't even remember much of what she said, and neither does she, but whatever she said about Dad made me cry for the first time that day. She ended with reiterating his three messages in life: be happy, be nice, and keep on trekking, the three things I live by each day of my life.

Be happy, because that is all you can do in life. It is what my dad would tell me on a daily basis. It takes too much energy to be angry all the time. Be nice, because being nice to others is the only thing that brings meaning to our lives. After all, if you are not kind to others, you will not be happy, because only people, not more money or more "stuff," bring happiness. She challenged us to go out and perform an act of kindness in memory of my dad. And finally, keep on trekking, because even when life gets tough, even when you are faced with situations that aren't fair and that you should never have to face, there is always someone out there who has it worse than you do. There is always a reason to keep on living, to keep climbing the mountain, because when you get to the top, the view truly is spectacular. If my dad could still climb the stairs when it took him the same energy as a normal person sprinting up and down ten times with a hundred-pound weight belt, then I could make it through the school day without falling asleep, do that one last routine at gymnastics practice, and finish my homework late at night. If my dad could keep a positive attitude when he was given some of the worst cards available, then I could too, no matter what cards I was dealt.

* * * * *

When I was five years old or so I would wake up every Saturday morning at eight to watch cartoons with my dad. For two hours, once a week, we would curl up on the couch in the upstairs TV room and watch *Timothy Goes To School, Seven Little Monsters, Marvin the Tap-Dancing Horse,* and *George Shrinks*. I thought I was the luckiest girl in the world for having a dad who always wanted to watch my favorite shows with me.

Each show lasted thirty minutes (and had no commercials too — the beauty of public television!) and had a basic plot that always kept the attention of a typical five-year-old. But within the quirky story lines always lay a moral of a message of some kind. My dad and I would often talk about them after and he would ask me what I had learned.

One of the lessons my dad would always come back to was from *Timothy Goes to School*. In the episode, Frank #1 and Frank #2, two twin Boston Terriers, accidentally break their classmate's toy helicopter rotor. They go home to tell their dad, Big Frank, what had happened at school that day. Big Frank tells them they need to apologize, but that apologizing is not just saying words.

Big Frank tells them they have to go through the Three Sorries. The first Sorry is to say you're sorry. The second Sorry is to feel you're sorry. And the third Sorry is to do something to show you're sorry. Big Frank said there was no option for them — they would need to complete the Three Sorries.

So the next day at school, Frank #1 and Frank #2 went up to their friend and told them they were sorry for breaking her toy. They also told her they felt sorry too — because they did. Then they went home and asked Big Frank for help to do something to show they were sorry. Big Frank said the only thing they could do was to replace their friend's toy. But they did even more than that. With the help of Big Frank, they made helicopter rotors not only for their friend, but for the entire class too. With that, they had completed the Three Sorries, a full apology to their friend for breaking her toy.

It is so easy to apologize for something and not mean it. I do it to my mom all the time — she tells me I forgot to do my dishes and I say I'm sorry, but do I really mean it? For the longest time after we watched that episode, my dad would always refer to the Three Sorries when I needed to apologize for something. Eventually, probably as a result of my telling him to stop treating me like a little kid and always referring to a stupid cartoon, he resorted to just telling me I needed to mean it when I apologized. But deep down, even if I didn't carry through with all the parts, I always thought of the Three Sorries.

I never quite understood why my dad was so "obsessed," as I would call it, with this concept. It is only after he died that I realized it was because this lesson falls in line with his three messages in life. A thorough apology is all about being kind to the person you've hurt. If you don't mean it and you don't act like it when you say you're sorry, you are not being kind to that person. If you complete the Three Sorries, you also feel better about yourself because you have done the right thing and corrected what you have done wrong, i.e. being happy. And finally, as my dad would always remind me, it's easy to say you're sorry, it's harder to actually feel you're sorry — like, deep down, so deep that you'll never do it again—and it's even harder still to do something to show you're sorry. But a thorough apology is not complete until you finish all three steps. No matter how hard it may be, no matter how much you don't want to admit you were in the wrong and approach the person you hurt, you must follow through and finish it, because after all, it is all about trekking on in life.

Chapter Nine
Wednesday, October 9th, 2013

When I woke up the day after the funeral, I felt somehow as if the play button in life had finally been pressed. I told myself it was finally going to be a normal day again, a normal day of going to school then gymnastics then coming home to do homework. I got up at 6:15 a.m., contemplated, as usual, what to wear, brushed my teeth, and went downstairs to eat my oatmeal. It was the start of any other normal day. Only it wasn't. Because my dad wasn't there.

That morning marked the first day I had only one parent to kiss goodbye before I walked out the door. It was the first day I didn't text my mom to ask if my dad was having a bad day. It was the first day I didn't have my phone glued to my pocket, waiting for a call from my mom telling me something had happened with dad. It was the first day I walked through the doors of my school as "that" girl whose dad had just died.

I certainly didn't know how to act when I got there, whether to appear sad and reserved or peppy and normal, pretending as though nothing had happened. Even more, I had no idea how other people were going to act when I saw them. I wanted to turn to someone and ask how you do it, show up like that and suddenly be the person who everyone feels the need to smile at, the person in the situation everyone is grateful that they are not in. The trouble was, I had no one to ask. I didn't know anyone who had a parent who had recently died.

I had seen friends every day since the day my dad died, and at the funeral the day before I saw many people from school, but that was when I was in my little bubble. The night before, I went to a boys' home soccer game where all the players and the people in the stands wore red in honor of my dad and ALS, which was wonderful and certainly made me tear up seeing all those people giving their support, but I still considered that "safe territory." I knew most of the people there, and my mom and uncle had even showed up halfway through. Going to school constituted being out in the real world, facing people I didn't really know and teachers who had piles of assignments stacked up from the time I had been out.

People always want to do the things in life that they know they cannot do because, well, the forbidden seems that much more attractive. Example: Since I can't eat gluten, freshly baked bread always looks that much more delicious, even though I never really liked bread when I could eat it; I only started to crave it once I knew I couldn't have it. When my dad first died, I wanted more than anything to go back to school and continue on with normal life, but I couldn't. The trouble is, when I was allowed to go back to school, all I wanted to do was curl up in a ball on the couch and watch TV all day long, continuing to live in my bubble. But I couldn't.

So I walked through those double doors of the high school and the first person I saw was my friend Anna, who also happened to be my teammate from gymnastics. She was wearing all red. From accidentally stalking my mom's email and looking at all those sympathy messages, I knew that Ms. Magnuson told people to wear red in honor of my dad and ALS awareness on the day that I got back to school, but whenever anyone had tried to organize a day for people to wear a certain color in the past, it never quite worked out. People forgot while others chose not to participate.

Anna grabbed my hand and walked me to the downstairs common area. I put my hand over my mouth. I was about to cry. Everyone—and I don't just mean my friends and casual acquaintances—*everyone*, including teachers, was wearing red. And for most people it wasn't just a hat or a bracelet—they had gone full out. People covered in red head to toe filed in and out of that room, face paint and red hearts, even on teachers, a common appearance.

People were staring at me as I walked in, taking note of the fact that I had finally returned, but it didn't even matter. I stopped along the hall and talked to lots of friends and then headed straight to Ms. Magnuson's room where I got one of the biggest hugs of my life (no joke). At that point I think I actually was in tears. Ninety-nine percent of the entire school was wearing red to show their love and support for my family and me, all because of her.

I think that's what ultimately made coming back so much easier than I had originally thought. These people didn't even have to say anything for me to know that they were thinking of me, that they were here for me. And because of this, there were no awkward encounters, no one who came up to me that I didn't know very well to say, "I'm really sorry for your loss," as I had been fearing. I didn't want to turn into "that" girl everyone felt sorry for and felt as though they needed to go up to and talk with to do their "good deed" of the day. A picture is worth a thousand words, and that picture in my mind of walking in and seeing everyone wearing red was far more meaningful than anything anyone could have said to me.

After I had initially crossed into the hub of everything, the day seemed ordinary. I went to class, turned in a bit of work that I had done (although all teachers told me not to worry about due dates or anything), and had lunch with my friends, joking about the normal stuff that teenagers do these days. I undoubtedly got waves of sadness throughout the day, but scores of people gave me hugs at times where I seemed to need it the most.

Even though the transition back to school went smoothly, I was still overwhelmed by the number of people who said, "Please let me know if there's anything I can do to help." It had come to the point where people just didn't know what to do. I didn't really get it until the funeral, but my mom, Kathryn, and I weren't the only ones feeling sad here. My grandparents and aunts and uncles, my dad's co-workers, family friends, and even my friends, had all cried at the funeral along with us, all sad and distraught over seeing someone they loved die and seeing two young girls and a mom in a position alone, without their father and husband.

It was heartwarming knowing that so many people were there to support us, but I still felt as though I was in a place where I had already been sad for a long time anyway and didn't need to grieve anymore. As I said before though, having a sick father is a very different thing from a dead father, and I didn't understand that at the time. I didn't think I had the right to be sad, because we had known he was going to die. I didn't know how to ask people for help or lean on them for support, because I had already navigated life alone when I found out my dad was sick, and I thought my only option was to cry alone. No matter how much I tried, it was still easier to revert to my default emotionless state, which seemed to work pretty well for me the entire day at school. Things changed when I went to gymnastics.

The last time I had been at the gym had been exactly one week ago when I sprinted out of practice, coming out with the news that my dad had died. Due to the nature of the sport, it's not ideal to be out of gymnastics for a week;

you come back uncoordinated and not as strong as when you left. Practice was going surprisingly well until around six, for all of a sudden I thought about what had been happening exactly one week ago. The EMTs and police officers had been at my house. My mom's world had come crashing down. And I had been at gymnastics, oblivious to everything going on. One week ago my dad had died. I kept saying it to myself, but no matter how many times I said it, it didn't seem any more real. It still seemed like he was just on a vacation or business trip and would be returning any day. But he wouldn't be coming back. All the emotions piled up on me and I started to get all shaky during my beam routine. I would never hear his voice again or feel the warmth in his hands. It was the first Hump Day without Dad.

I couldn't do it anymore. I jumped off the beam, tears in my eyes, and went over to my coach. She knew exactly what I was going to say as soon as I walked up to her. One week ago she was the one who had told me my mom was here and that I had to leave. One week ago she saw me break down in the locker room, blaming myself for getting my dad sick. She sent me home and told me just to be with my family and get a good night's rest. The physical and mental demands of gymnastics were too much for me. Instead of resting though, I went home and poured myself into my schoolwork. Unlike gymnastics, schoolwork is easy. It is straightforward and I don't run the risk of snapping a bone if I mess up. So I sat there and wrote my lab report, practiced math problems, and read *As I Lay Dying* (the worst book in existence, by the way), and I stayed busy. I didn't let my mind wander. I forgot about life for the moment.

The next few days seemed normal and gymnastics practice went as well as ever. But then the next Wednesday rolled around, marking two weeks since my dad died. And once again, at around 6:00 p.m., I had another meltdown. I held back the tears this time; it was just sadness, sadness that consumed me and made me feel weak. And so I went home and, once again, dove right into my schoolwork. I didn't want to talk to my mom or anyone. The constant replay of the events of Wednesday October 2nd haunted me every Wednesday, the constant reminder to me of how many weeks it had been since I had seen my dad.

It took me a few weeks to finally make it through a Wednesday gymnastics practice. I think it was probably Emma who snapped me out of my weekly spiral of doom when she finally told me that the whole Wednesday thing was not helping me in the long run. She said she knew it sounded harsh and immediately followed with a bunch of confidence boosters and whatnot, but she was absolutely right. This was exactly what I needed to hear. For the second time in the past year I woke up, picking myself up from the gym floor this time, and realized that Wednesday is just another ordinary day. There was no reason for me to be sadder on a Wednesday than on a Friday.

Overall, I began to bounce back to my usual peppy self, but there were of course moments where something would trigger me and I would suddenly get sad. I remember one time seeing a mom and dad walking through the mall with their teenage girls, thinking to myself that that will never again be us. Another time, I was watching a movie in school about a man miraculously living with a disease that caused all his muscles to atrophy away, and tears of despair began to run down my face as I questioned how it could be possible for this man to be alive at sixty pounds and yet my dad, much stronger and more independent the day he died, couldn't. These trigger moments showed up here and there in the months following my dad's death, but I was told they were normal. I was supposed to be sad. I was supposed to start crying randomly sometimes.

I am definitely a person of extremes, a person of black or white. Either I drink coffee or I don't drink coffee; I do my homework well or I don't do it at all. My mom and I always argue about this ("You can have one cup of coffee per day, just not seven"), but if I can't have or do something to the fullest extent, what is the point of doing it at all? It is easier for me to just eliminate something entirely. So with Wednesdays, once I told myself I wasn't going to cry at six anymore, it didn't happen again. I'm not sure if that was a good or a bad thing, but that was what happened.

Week by week, I began to relax a bit more, the fake smile turning into a real smile or, at times, simply a face of sadness and despair. It's easy to think that people who just lost their mom or dad might be sad when talking about them, but for me, talking about my dad, talking about memories and the things he would always tell me, made me feel better. Maybe that's one of the reasons I decided I wanted to continue fighting ALS even after my dad died. Or maybe it was because I wanted to be proactive. I knew nothing I did would bring my dad back, but maybe I would be able to influence the lives of those in the future who have this awful disease. Maybe I could find a reason as to why my dad died.

And with that, I embarked on my journey to increase awareness of ALS more than ever. With the ALS Walk and my dad's passing, the name ALS suddenly became a more common term in my small hometown of Falmouth, Maine. You would think that a disease that is currently one-hundred percent fatal would have scientists all over it, racing to be the person who would be acclaimed for finding its cure. But, somehow, ALS is still an "orphan disease," a disease that not many people have, not many people know about, and not many people choose to direct funds towards to help make progress on a cure.

Looking back on the previous paragraph, notice how I said ALS is *currently* one-hundred percent fatal. *Currently* is the key word: ALS is not incurable; it is simply underfunded.

Private drug companies are most likely not the answer for a cure for ALS. Quickly progressing diseases such as ALS are less attractive to drug companies because they know making a profit will be harder. It can take over fifteen years and over one billion dollars to develop a new drug for ALS, and the chances of producing a drug that is successful is low; ninety-nine percent of drugs tested failed to work or even make it to the clinical trial phase. Due to these difficulties, there is little opportunity for private drug companies to make money even if they did find a potential cure. Private companies would have more opportunity for profit by developing drugs for diseases that a person can use throughout his or her life, such as insulin for diabetics.

Private companies often simply do not have the resources to pursue a drug to target ALS patients. Even if a drug is found that is successful in targeting ALS, private companies have the ability to charge whatever amount they choose for it. Rilutek, the drug my dad was on, is currently the only FDA-approved drug to prolong the life of someone with ALS, but it is not a cure; it only extends life by an average of three months. Furthermore, Rilutek costs $2,035 per month, and is not always covered by insurance. While the progress of drug companies is very slow, people afflicted by this disease continue to decline rapidly, just waiting for a cure.

Then there is governmental funding. However, the National Institutes of Health (NIH) reported in 2013 only $39 million of governmental funding was allocated to ALS. Part of the reason funding is limited for ALS is that there is a limited population of people who have this disease.

Compared to the one in every 50,000 people in the United States diagnosed with ALS every year, one in eight people is diagnosed with Alzheimer's and one in eight women is diagnosed with breast cancer. These staggering numbers are a function of the funding for these respective diseases: in 2013 the NIH reported $566 million given to Alzheimer's and $763 million to breast cancer.

There are many initiatives that are currently trying to increase governmental funding for ALS, but as we all know too well, Congress moves slowly. Bills that are presented have a good chance of not even making it past the committee, and even if they do proceed and are well liked, it can take years before they are enacted and actually enforced.

So what would happen if we could change ALS's orphan disease status? In the United States, an orphan disease is defined as a disease that affects fewer than 200,000 people at a given time, and obviously we don't want the current statistic of 30,000 people living with ALS to increase. However, an orphan disease can also be defined as a disease that is not well known, making research into a cure insufficient. This is the angle I decided to take.

Relying on private companies to spend their resources slowly developing a treatment for ALS and waiting for Congress to act may not be the most promising way to go in the quest for a cure for ALS. However, the more people who know about this disease, the more people who could donate money to organizations like the ALS Association to help fund research.

* * * * *

Late October 2013

It was actually my friend Amy who gave me the idea for the bracelets. With the success of the Red Trekkers bracelets at the Walk, she thought we might be able to sell some bracelets around the school. She came up with the slogan, "Keep Calm and Trek On." Yes, it was a spin off of the old British war saying and just about every other copy of it, but it couldn't have been more in line with my dad's message in life. When things get tough, stay calm. When he would start coughing or choking uncontrollably, he needed to learn to just stay calm and it would pass. When life got stressful and doctors couldn't give us any answers, we just needed to take a deep breath. Ultimately, we just needed to keep trekking.

Don't get me wrong, though—some things we just couldn't stay calm about, like the fact that my dad's breathing was cut in half in a matter of months or he that was dropping weight every single day. When people would tell me, albeit with the best intentions, "It'll all be okay," and, "I know," when I would tell them what was going on with Dad, I could feel the anger bubbling inside me. No, it would not be okay. I didn't care what anyone said. There was exactly zero hope that my dad would get any better. People could try to empathize, but unless they had watched a parent slowly die right in front of their eyes, there was no way they could understand.

In the end though, no matter how quickly my dad deteriorated, if there was one thing I would change, it would have been to stop planning for the future. We reached a point, probably that summer right before he died, where we knew we didn't have much time left. Still, we were planning what we would be doing the following week rather than what we would be doing that day. We would be worrying about what his breathing would be like three months from now rather than what it was like that day.

Planning was our way of trying to keep calm. But ultimately, in the last few weeks of his life here on Earth, we realized keeping calm meant taking a deep breath and not worrying about what was out of our control. We couldn't change the fact that his breathing was deteriorating every day. My dad was dying of ALS and there was nothing we could do. From the beginning, my dad accepted the fact that there was no use trying to be mad at someone or something for this turn of events, and we had to learn how to follow his lead in this way of thinking. This was not what we had planned on, but then again, how can you ever plan for life? In the end, even though my dad left us much earlier than we had anticipated, we kept calm and continued moving along in life. Even up until the end, we tried to live as normal a life as possible. Because sometimes that's all you can do. Trek On.

Once Amy gave me the idea, I immediately ordered eight hundred red bracelets that said Keep Calm and Trek On, marking the beginning of my quest to spread awareness of ALS and fundraise for a cure. As soon as they arrived, my friends and I hung posters up around the school advertising that we would be giving them away at lunch, with a donation strongly suggested.

Quick business tip I learned: if you say something is one dollar, people will give you one dollar. If you say it's five dollars, people might be turned off and not want to buy one. That was not the goal; we ultimately wanted as many people as possible to wear them to spread awareness of ALS, and raising money was a bonus. However, if you say you get something if you make a donation to an organization such as the ALS Association, then you'll have people lining up. Key word: *get*, not *buy*. People like to get free stuff, and when there is no set amount, people will be more attracted to the product and will feel as though they are being a good person when they give more than a few dollars.

My friend Louisa and I set up camp during lunch on a Monday. We had a plastic table, a sign, a cashbox, and a basket full of bracelets. The sign, as well as signs all over the school, read: "Bracelets for ALS Research in Memory of Jim Caldwell." Everyone knew Jim Caldwell was my dad. Everyone knew he'd died of ALS. With the posters in the school from the Walk, I made it okay for someone to come forward and say, "My dad is sick." With the posters for these bracelets, I made it okay for someone to openly discuss and pay tribute to a deceased parent. I made it okay not to bury what happened. Even back to Ms. Magnuson's organizing the entire school to wear red, my dad's death set a precedent for a school to reach out to a person who had just lost his or her parent. Because even though it was my dad who died, the hearts of those who didn't even know us ached as they looked at their own fathers and imagined what life would be like if the tables were turned, if, by some stroke of bad luck, they came home one day to a house without their dad.

But still, as we set up the table in the cafeteria, I didn't know if people would actually buy the bracelets. Most of the people in my close circle of friends had already gotten a bracelet. For all I knew, all other people at lunch would think I was some crazy, depressed girl who was trying to channel her sadness by getting random people to buy these bracelets. So I was shocked when the first person who came up was a guy from my math class I had never actually talked with before. He gave five dollars. A teacher I never had walked by and gave a donation. An entire lunch table got up, each person throwing in a few dollars. As lunch ended, a frenzy of people rushed up to us, each throwing bills onto the table as they picked up a bracelet and went to class.

We sold bracelets at lunch all week long, and even after that, I had people coming up to me daily asking if they could still get one. In the next several months, I had people hand out bracelets to anyone they knew, and wherever I went I brought some. I stopped asking for donations because I just wanted to distribute them to as many people as possible. Soon, people from coast to coast were wearing Red Trekkers bracelets and giving them to all their friends as well. And they weren't just wearing them the first day they got them — people, even months later, still wore a red bracelet every single day.

To this day, I look at the people I would least expect to be wearing a bracelet all these months later, and I want to tear up whenever I see that flash of red on their wrist. The writing is sometimes faded and the vibrant red color slightly dull, but every single morning when they put that bracelet on (or don't take it off for that matter), even if they aren't thinking about it, they are reminded of ALS. Because of me, because of Dad, they are wearing it. But it's not just about supporting my family anymore — it is supporting anyone who has been affected by ALS.

After a few months, bracelet donations had totaled $700. In the whole scheme of things, it's not a lot. $700 may not be the key to finding a cure for ALS, and it is nothing compared to the millions of dollars that get donated to the cause, but how many million dollar donations does the ALS Association consistently get? Not many. $700 will buy 17,500 plastic pipettes to draw fluids and chemicals that might be key in a treatment for ALS. $700 will buy 230 glass Petri dishes to watch cultured cells grow in as someone tries to find out what actually causes motor neurons to die in a person with ALS. And $700 will help contribute to the steep price tag of a piece of equipment that is needed and would not be made possible without donations like this.

But perhaps the most important aspect of these bracelets is their power to increase awareness of ALS. I keep saying it, I know, but before my dad was diagnosed with ALS, not many people in our family, town, or close circle of friends knew what ALS was. They might have known it was a bad disease, but I rarely came across a person who knew that it is a neurological disease, that a person with ALS can feel things and has a perfectly alert mind but can't move, and that the life expectancy is, on average, three to five years after diagnosis. Most people did not know that there is no effective cure or treatment.

But at least in my hometown of Falmouth, Maine, this has all changed due to our advocacy. Whenever I give out a bracelet, I tell people these basic facts, and as a result, if you asked a random person in my high school or in my town what ALS is, there's a good chance they will be able to tell you something more than, "it's a disease."

Still, just because more people know about ALS doesn't mean we are any closer to finding a cure. This is especially evident given the fact that, in the grand scheme of things, I've only "spread the word" to several thousand people or so. However, the more people who know about this disease and the more attention we can draw toward it, the more people who will want to donate to the cause, a fact that is especially evident with the ALS Ice Bucket Challenge that swept the nation the following year.

Whenever I tell someone about ALS, I get the same look of shock and dismay, people telling me they had no idea how bad a disease it is and wanting to know what they can do to help. I tell them they can make a donation to help fund ALS research, and that is exactly what they do. Even if I just met the person and I'm giving him or her a bracelet because I want to tell them about ALS, the poignancy of my story makes them eager to open their wallet and give a few dollars. And, as you can see from the numbers above, even a nickel can make a difference — I know that sounds crazy, but a nickel buys one and a quarter plastic pipettes, and maybe those pipettes will be key in developing a treatment for ALS.

* * * * *

I remember when I was younger I knew a girl whose mom had died, and whenever I was around her I was very careful not to mention my mom at all. I didn't want to say anything that might upset her or make her wish her mom was still alive. But I talk about my dad all the time. Within twenty-four hours of meeting anyone, I guarantee they will know at least three things about me: I drink too much coffee, I always have to pee (because of all the coffee!), and my dad recently died from ALS.

So back to that look of "shock and dismay" people give me when I describe ALS. Part of that response might be because whenever I give someone a bracelet I always lead with, "My dad recently died" in a nonchalant and peppy type of way, a type of way that leaves people doing a double take and immediately responding with, "Oh my gosh I'm so sorry."

Now, I get that I do have the tendency to spring this news upon people. One time a girl I had just met asked me what my necklace was, and I responded with, "Oh, my dad died a few months ago and my necklace is an engraving of his thumbprint." Another time, when talking with someone and he asked if my mom was married, I responded with, "Well, my dad just died, so I guess no." That poor kid looked like he was about to pass out when I said that. Nice going on my part, I know. I hadn't meant for it to sound as sarcastic and lighthearted as it came out, and I felt awful for spilling the news to him like that. I just reached a point where I kind of went on autopilot when it came to telling my story.

It has been less than a year since my dad died. I probably shouldn't act or feel the way I do, insisting that I am okay and talking about the fact that my dad died like it is no big deal, but for some reason, I do it anyway. I talk about him in the present tense, telling people that my dad hates olives, just like me, and that he loves to play golf but somehow I didn't inherit that passion. I tell stories about him on a regular basis and discuss all his annoying little traits in a nonchalant manner, like how he always felt the need to remind me of what time it is every night, his subtle yet obnoxious way of telling me I need to go to bed right then, or else.

Perhaps one of my worst moments was when I was telling someone how my dad and I had always planned on going scuba diving in Australia when I graduated from high school but that now it probably wouldn't be possible, and when he innocently asked why, I bluntly responded, albeit with a smile, "My dad died. He's dead. We can't do it anymore." The kid turned bright red. He knew my dad had died and just hadn't been thinking in that moment. He didn't know what to say. Well, I don't blame him—I wouldn't either if I were in that situation.

The room went silent for a few moments, a sly grin across my face because I thought what I had just said was the funniest thing ever. "Sarah, we don't know when you're kidding and when you're not," my friend soberly said. To me, it was okay to joke about the fact that my dad had died and put others on the spot. But these others were not only left on the spot, they were left with sinkholes in their stomachs, with feelings of guilt and remorse, just waiting for me to burst out sobbing.

But I didn't start sobbing. Instead, I held a sense of satisfaction, a sense of power, because I could talk about my dad in any way I wanted — I could tell stories about him all day long and make people feel guilty every day if I wanted — because I was in control. It goes back to the whole thing during my concussion where I would only eat oatmeal and chicken because it was my way of controlling at least something in my life when I had no power over all the things that were going wrong in my life — I always wanted to be in control. No one was going to tell me to shut up or to stop being insensitive because then it would make them seem insensitive.

I made the calls as to when I wanted to bring my dad up, and because of that, I was able to talk only about what I wanted to, and no one would pry me for information; they would just let me say what I was going to say. Now, of course there are exceptions. I would often have heart to heart discussions with some of my closest friends, but once again, I would usually be the one offering up the information. A friend may have asked how I was doing, but unless I wanted to go down the emotional path and discuss how I was *really* doing, how I missed my dad so much I didn't even want to admit it, I didn't have to. I could continue going down the path of, "I'm doing fine."

And that is exactly what I did, starting on day one with that email to Ms. Magnuson about how my dad was "in a better place." A few days after he died, I went to Holly's house and was talking to her and Louisa for a while when Louisa's brother came over. He gave me a hug and told me he was really sorry about my dad. "Thank you, I'm okay though. He's in a better place, and he looked so peaceful," I automatically said.

"Well, that doesn't make it any easier," he told me. I paused, smiled, and then forgot about what he said. But even to this day, I still remember that response like it was yesterday. He was right, and it took me five months to realize it.

* * * * *

March 20th, 2014

Ms. Magnuson warned me. She was the one who had told me a breakdown was on the brink. She was the one who reminded me I couldn't keep my act going on forever.

Lots of times if I don't have a class or have nothing else to do, I just wander off to Ms. Magnuson's room. It's my "home base," the place I automatically go to when I walk into school in the morning. It was the first room I set foot in as a freshman where she introduced herself as Amy Magnuson, "the advisor you are stuck with for the next four years whether you like it or not." One of the very first things out of her mouth was, "I'm a very sarcastic person." Just the way she said it made me like her immediately. I went home that day and told my mom I really liked my advisor because "she's cool."

For the first two years of high school I camped out in her room every now and then, but I didn't spend much time with her other than advisory, the short period we all agree is a great excuse to waste time and forget about whatever survey we're supposed to be doing as a group. So instead, we would talk about strange biology-related things (like the fact that dolphins have sex for pleasure), and she would show us videos of her two young boys, one naming all the players on the Red Sox team and the other doing something destructive. I knew I liked her, and I knew I wanted to take AP Biology with her junior year, but I didn't give much thought beyond the fact that was sarcastic (i.e. funny) and that was cool.

Going into junior year, she knew my dad had ALS because I sent an email to all my teachers telling them about the Walk and asking them to donate (which she of course did). On one of the first days of school, somehow the Walk and my dad's illness came up when I was talking to her briefly, and she reminded me she knows what it's like. No, her dad had not been sick, but her mom had; no, it wasn't ALS, but it was rapidly progressing throat cancer; and no, she was not sixteen, but she was twenty-four. At age sixteen you're supposed to be visiting colleges with your dad, not watching him die right before your eyes; at age twenty-four you're supposed to be calling your mom every other day to update her on your new job, not to make sure she's not in the hospital.

So she gets it. She gets what it's like to have a dying parent, to be "that" person everyone feels bad for. And so she would just talk to me, transforming from a funny teacher full of dry humor to a soft-spoken friend who not only talked to me about my life, but added input about her own as well. She told me life isn't fair and that there's no sense in trying to figure out why these things happened to me.

After my dad died, she told me I wasn't supposed to go back to my normal life and be okay; I wasn't supposed to talk about his death like it was something that happened years ago. I was supposed to ask for extensions on assignments and miss a day of school here and there. She told me I needed to take some time to feel sad, because that was what I was supposed to feel. She told me I wasn't okay, and I probably wouldn't be okay in a month or six months or even a year, because I would still be a bit sad for the rest of my life.

On one particular afternoon in March, I found myself in Ms. Magnuson's classroom during one of her free periods. We were just talking about a bunch of random things, and somehow the topic of my dad came up. She reminded me, once again, that I couldn't keep going the way I was. She knew, as I did, that whenever I would tell my story I would go into autopilot mode and recite a script that I had come to memorize. She knew that defense mode all too well herself.

In order to be okay, I needed to find meaning in my father's dying when I was sixteen years old. And so, the week after he died, I dove head first into the ALS campaign. I gave his death a purpose: I was going to help others with ALS.

I knew nothing I could do for ALS sufferers would bring my dad back, but helping others in my dad's situation could keep him alive to me. If what I did could save these other people, it was almost as if I were saving my dad too. Saving others almost made it more okay that he died.

I tell my story to people and they tell me I am an incredible and selfless person. I smile and tell them I am just trying to carry on my dad's legacy, and maybe one day, make it so that a father with two young girls who was just diagnosed with ALS will be able to smile as they graduate from high school, cry when they graduate from college, and bawl his eyes out as he walks them down the aisle on their wedding day.

So that day with Ms. Magnuson, as I sat on a table, staring out the window and watching the melting snow on the ground, she once again told me I am an incredible person, a direct reflection of who my dad was. She told me he is watching over me and wants me to continue enjoying my life and being the shining star he helped create. But she also told me I was going to wake up one day and suddenly all the emotions I had been concealing for the past five months were going to come flooding out.

She had watched as my stress levels began rising between school and gymnastics. She had watched as the days had passed and I still had yet to face the reality: my dad was not coming back. I had said it over and over again, but there's a difference between saying something and really *knowing* it.

I stared out the window and watched a bird peck at a bush just beneath my gaze. I didn't want to accept what Ms. Magnuson was saying. I thought to myself how easy it must be to be a bird. I told myself I was okay; I told her I was okay. But she, once again, told me I wasn't, and deep down, I knew it too.

Later that afternoon, I tried to think of the last time I cried. Like, really cried. The summer I found out my dad was sick, I cried every day as I thought about the fact that I wouldn't get to grow up with him by my side. As the months passed, I cried as I saw him growing weaker every day, right before my eyes. When he started getting even worse, I cried out of anger and frustration and resentment toward this disease. And when he died, I cried out of pure heartbreak, the pit-in-your-stomach feeling that makes you feel as though you cannot move. But then the tears stopped. I don't know when—probably that Wednesday when I decided I wasn't going to cry anymore—but they stopped. And on that day in March, I could not remember the last time I had cried.

This is what I was thinking about at gymnastics practice. I remember standing there, just staring at the uneven bars, frozen. I was supposed to be doing my routine, but I couldn't move. I was thinking about what Ms. Magnuson had told me. It was the last practice before States, one of the highest-stress level meets of the year. I needed a certain score in order to qualify for Regionals; if I fell just once on any of the four events, there was a good chance I wouldn't make it. I thought about my dad again. It would be the first time I would have a state gymnastics meet and he wouldn't be there. It would be the first time he wouldn't come in early to help set up the gym for hosting the competition. I thought about how easy it was to fall on beam, how easy it was not to make it to Regionals. I thought about the fact that I would never hear my dad's voice again, never see his smiling face again.

Tears started to flood my eyes. I didn't know what was happening to me. It was my turn to go. I needed to start moving. I did my routine and fell on one of the release moves from low bar to high bar. Tears streamed down my face even more. I had only cried four times at gymnastics in my entire life: three from bad injuries and one in the locker room when I knew something had happened to my dad. I finished my routine and my coach asked if I was okay. I said I was fine and that I wasn't actually crying; I suppose that probably wasn't the best statement I could've made because I soon started hyperventilating, my eyes bright red and my face wet from tears.

I told myself I couldn't stop training though. I needed to keep going. I did another routine. And I fell. Again. My bars coach called me over, not even making me finish. He didn't really know what to do with me; I don't think he had ever seen me cry. He again asked what was wrong. I said I was just tired. He didn't buy it. I'm sure he knew it was more than that, maybe putting the pieces together that it had something to do with my dad. He said I needed to go home because it wasn't safe for me to be doing gymnastics. I told him I couldn't go home; it was the practice before States. He told me if I could convince the other coach, the coach who had held me as I cried in the locker room five months ago, that I was fine, then I could stay. I knew there was no chance of that.

I went upstairs to the locker room, sat on the bench, put my head on my bent knees, and started sobbing. I couldn't stop thinking about my dad. I didn't even know why I was crying, but the more I wondered why I was so sad or angry or whatever I was, the more the tears came. I realized Ms. Magnuson was right. Nothing I could do would bring my dad back. I wasn't okay. I was sad and angry and confused and I missed my dad more than I could put into words.

Emma, Anna, and a few other girls came upstairs. I imagine I probably looked like a federal emergency with my splotchy red tear-covered face and disheveled hair. No matter what anyone said to me though, the tears would not stop. I reached a point where I suddenly couldn't catch my breath. I got scared. I had finally allowed myself to feel the pain and sorrow that I should have felt all those months ago. And all those feelings I chose to ignore and gloss over as I focused my energy on other people with ALS and tried to forget about my dad suddenly came out. I couldn't control the emotions and the crying no matter how hard I tried to stop. I realized it was like my dad must have felt, his body not doing what he wanted it to. I cried even harder.

Eventually I had no more tears that could come out. Anna went downstairs and affirmatively told the coaches I was going home, as in saying Sarah is so bad right now that there is no negotiation no matter what you say or what she tells you. Emma just sat with me, not saying anything at all, and when I finally pulled myself together, we went downstairs. I went over to my coach and she gave me a hug, not even asking for an explanation. I couldn't imagine what she was thinking—one of her top-level gymnasts was an emotional wreck the practice before the most important meet of the year, not stable enough to do gymnastics at the moment. The younger kids she was coaching came over and asked what was wrong. What was I supposed to tell them? I was having a nervous breakdown?

When I was younger, I always thought of the older girls as unbreakable and perfect, never crying or getting angry. Now, I'm that older girl, and that's how these kids see me. I'm one of the people they all look up to, the person who is a leader in the group and always gives them advice when they are scared or nervous. In their eyes, I am perfect.

When they asked, I just kind of smiled for a few moments, not sure what to say. I ended up telling them I was just really tired and hadn't been getting much sleep (which was true). I expected them to ask more questions, but they didn't. One of the girls came over and gave me a huge hug—and didn't let go. Then all the others followed and joined in on the big group hug, everyone wanting to have a turn to hug me individually. My heart melted. Sometimes it's the little things in life that make all the difference.

When I went home I curled up on the couch with my two dogs and fell asleep. In that moment, nothing in life mattered anymore. I didn't think about the schoolwork I had to do for the next day, finally using Ms. Magnuson's "free pass" offer with all my teachers. I didn't think about the gymnastics meet in two days. I didn't even think about my dad much. I just thought about my dogs.

Whether scientific evidence backs it up or not, anyone who has ever owned a dog can attest to the fact that they have some sort of sixth sense that allows them to know when something is wrong. When my mom was going through her cancer surgeries and radiation, Keeley would just stare at her for hours and hours, never having done that before. She would follow my mom around wherever she went and would never want to be alone. When my dad got sick, it was Finnegan who wouldn't leave his side.

But the weirdest incident of all happened the night my dad died. Keeley and Finnegan normally bark like crazy and sprint through the house whenever the doorbell rings or someone comes through the door. They get even worse whenever a loud car drives past or there are sirens in the distance. That night though, while dozens of people were coming in and out of the house, the doorbell ringing like crazy and sirens from the police cars and ambulance coming and going, the dogs didn't make a single noise. They didn't come out even once. It was only when we were sitting on the couch after things had quieted down that we realized they were MIA; we found them curled up in their kennels and had to drag them out so they could come sit with us. Call me crazy, but they knew something had happened.

When I got home from gymnastics that day and curled up on the couch, both Keeley and Finnegan jumped up and sat with me. They usually wouldn't do that; if one dog is on the couch, the other won't get on because neither of them likes to share my attention. But that day, both lay with me on the couch and looked into my eyes in a way that truly made me think they knew something was wrong. Once again, sometimes it is the small things that make all the difference. As I sat with them, curled up in a fuzzy blanket and away from the stress of gymnastics and the hype of school, my brain finally had a chance to calm down. I had finally given myself the time I needed to reflect on everything. Life had once again been put on pause, but this time I made sure I was ready before I pressed the play button again.

* * * * *

I went to bed at around eight that night. I was too exhausted to stay up anymore just staring at the wall or watching TV, but my mind kept racing and I couldn't force myself to fall asleep. I kept thinking about my dad. It was his empty seat at the table, the missing person in the car, his dusty golf bag sitting in the garage. My dad was not coming back. I kept telling it to myself. He was not going to be there for my gymnastics meet. He was not going to take me out to dinner or buy me candy after the meet like he always did. He was not going to annoy me when he asked for the seventeenth time what a certain skill in one of my routines is called. My dad was not coming back.

As much as my heart ached and I felt like crying yet again, I fell asleep. I fell asleep because I could dream. Dreaming is a funny thing; no matter how crazy the situation, in the moment it seems completely normal. For those few moments, the dream world is my reality.

I dream about my dad often. Sometimes we are going someplace together and other times I'm talking with him about something. I wish I could say I remember what we talk about and that he gives me some extraordinary advice that will change the way I live my life, or that I experience something with him that I know will never get to in real life, like graduating from high school, but I honestly don't remember much of these dreams at all. Most of the time he is simply there. I see snapshots of our family — the four of us. I see him walking along the golf course. I see his smile.

But I never see him with ALS. I see him running around with the dogs in the backyard, his legs strong and muscular. I see him swinging a golf club and hiking to the top of Mt. Katahdin, the highest mountain in Maine and the end of the Appalachian Trail. I see him riding the exercise bike and watching the news on full volume, then going to the floor to do sit ups, working on the six pack I always tell him he should have being such the skinny guy that he is. I watch him eating the lobsters he just brought back from a scuba diving trip with his buddies in Florida.

I see him the way I always remembered him. That is what he wanted most of all. He would always tell me he didn't want me to remember him as old and weak; he wanted me to remember him as the strong and energetic dad whose daughters were his world. As much as I hated seeing him get weaker and weaker and struggling to tie his shoes, button his shirt, and brush his teeth, no one hated it more than he. He wanted me to remember him taking care of me, not the other way around. Well, I guess I lived up to his wish—even in my unconscious state of mind.

* * * * *

I talked earlier about Elizabeth Kübler-Ross' *Five Stages of Grief*, describing my behavior after I found out my dad was sick. I discussed how I finally reached acceptance around a year after he was diagnosed with ALS. While the ensuing months of seeing my dad get worse were a rollercoaster of emotions, I had come to terms with our new "normal" and the fact that he was going to die far sooner than anyone wanted. But no matter how much I felt as though I had reached "acceptance," nothing could have prepared me for the day he died. It was one of those things that I knew was going to happen but never thought the day would actually come. And so I entered into a whole new realm of the *Five Stages of Grief*.

Denial. It was my form of self-defense, my way of being able to live in this world without my dad. Well, that was pretty much the entire time up until my breakdown at the end of March. While not exactly a medical term, a nervous breakdown is exactly what I decided to diagnose myself with. According to Wikipedia — yes, the most reliable source we have access to these days — a nervous breakdown results from "severe stress-induced depression, anxiety, or dissociation... often closely tied to psychological burnout, severe overwork, sleep deprivation, and similar stressors, which combine to temporarily overwhelm an individual." Sound like me? I thought so. And uncontrollable crying in the middle of gymnastics practice seems to be a plausible result.

Fortunately, this event brought me out of a huge cycle of denial, but that is not to say the denial was gone completely. Even one year later, I still talk about my dad like he is still here. I still tell stories of the stupid things he did when he was in his "crazy years" (quick digression: he jumped through a six foot bonfire over and over again and then fell right in it when he'd had one too many beers), and I still complain about the fact that he was too cheap to buy the "good" kind of milk at the grocery store (he *insisted* on buying the supermarket's brand because it is "just as good"). Is that denial? Maybe not, but it is still me transitioning between my dad being here on Earth and my dad being my guardian angel. It's as though I am stuck in that awkward phase of not knowing whether to talk about him in the present or in the past. Eventually, it will all switch to the past, but for now, I just like to keep him alive, because that is all I can do to prevent myself from going insane.

The thing is though, whenever I talk about my dad, it is always me offering up the information. Even as I describe the gruesome details of his ALS or as I look at both old pictures and pictures from right before he died, I don't shed a tear. However, it is instances when someone says to me, out of the blue, "We sure do miss your dad around here," or, "Your dad was a really great guy," that make me tear up.

Which brings me to the anger. I'm angry whenever people associate me with the girl who has the dead father, feeling the need to check in on me to see how I'm doing just so they can fulfill their Good Samaritan act of the day. I'm angry whenever anyone talks about my dad like they were best buds with him when they really only talked with him a handful of times. I'm angry when my dad's not there to help me edit my essays on politics or read my lab reports or when I don't have anyone to call to say it's okay for me to leave school when I'm not feeling well and my mom can't be reached. I'm angry when I see people living with ALS for years when my dad only made it sixteen months. I'm angry when I think of the things I wish I could have done differently with my time left with him, the apologies I should have said for all the times I was mean to him.

So there's the first glimpse of bargaining. Bargaining is the one that took form the most right after I found out my dad was sick—I promised I would never be mean or rude to him ever again if his diagnosis would somehow go away. Even after I knew the diagnosis was real and wouldn't go away, I still said I was going to be the perfect child if he would just get better. Needless to say, neither of those things happened.

Nowadays, whatever "bargaining" I do is just another form of resentment. I know there's nothing I, or anyone, for that matter, could have done to prevent my dad from getting ALS, but I still have resentment over the fact that I should have been a better daughter for his time here on Earth. I cringe when I think of the days where I wished he would just go on more business trips and when I would be angry when Tuesday night golf was canceled because I just wanted "Girl's Night," free from the annoyance of my father. Tuesday nights were our time to eat pancakes for dinner (okay, more frequently stir fry) while watching TV at the same time, a forbidden thing when my dad was around. Now, as my mom, Kathryn, and I sit around the kitchen table staring down the empty chair, it is Girl's Night every night, but the celebration of "free time" is long gone. Bargaining means wishing you could go back to the way things used to be, correcting everything you did wrong and saying the things you wish you had said. Bargaining is what I do every day.

Then there's depression. Fortunately, this stage for me has been the easiest to face only because I know how easy it is to fall into its trap. Without a doubt this is the stage that hit me the hardest after my dad got sick — after all, I dedicated a whole chapter to it. Of course, depression occurred the moment I found out my dad had died, the moment my world suddenly stopped. After the initial shock of his death and the week of numbness that followed, I was scared to let myself feel my emotions because I knew what that depression felt like. I knew oh too well the feeling of the stab in the heart, the stormy cloud following me around wherever I went, and it was a place I never wanted to go again. My strategy of masking my emotions worked better than ever. But then, on March 20th my little breakdown occurred, and suddenly denial wasn't working so well for me anymore. My wall of self-defense had finally come crashing down. I was sad and confused and angry all at the same time.

In some ways though, it is a relief that March 20th happened. It is a relief — for me and everyone else, I'm sure — knowing I'm not a ticking time bomb anymore. The day after it happened, I was still a bit shaken up, but by that Saturday, my brain was clear and I went into the gymnastics meet knowing that although my dad might not have been there in person, he was still watching. The mountain of stress dissolved. I had my best meet of the season and placed very well, a bonus.

Since March 20th, I have allowed myself time every night to be sad, just a little. Even if it was a great day and I don't feel sad at all, I still give myself a chance to cry. It's all about diffusing the bomb before it explodes. Some days I don't cry at all, and other days I cry multiple times during the day before I finally reach my pillow and fall asleep with the salty tears dripping down my cheeks. And since March 20th, every time I cry—whether it's a legitimate reason (i.e. missing my dad) or completely foolish (i.e. thinking my mom is completely unfair and ruining my life when she asks me to empty the dishwasher and we get into a fight)—I remind myself that I am not okay. And this time I mean it.

I suppose this is the closest I will get to acceptance, for now. Notice how I talk about all these stage of grief in the present tense—because I am still living them. I'm never going to be not in denial or not be angry or not try to bargain. There's a little part of me that's never going to be not depressed, and I'm never going to be "fine," because I have lost my dad, and that is something I will never get over. I still miss my father every waking minute, and that will never change.

Because I think of this almost every day, I'll go back to what Ms. Magnuson told me just twelve hours into the life I will learn to call normal: "There is no sense in any of this—it is tragic and unfair and there is no reason to any of this. Though at some point you will attempt to find reason and want some form of explanation, you may never get it. And that's okay because there may not have been a reason."

Acceptance means being able to move forward, but it does not mean forgetting. Sometimes when I'm home alone I open up my dad's drawers just to smell his clothes. The socks are still perfectly aligned, the flashlight that he always used to see through the darkness still working.

Everyone is put on Earth for a reason. I may never find a reason as to why he was taken from us too quickly, but I do know the reason he was put on Earth. His purpose was to raise his two daughters and turn them into wonderful young women. I recently found an old letter to myself from freshman year in high school, just three years ago. I said my dad had taught me patience and compassion towards others, which is perfectly in line with his three most important things to remember in life that I later spelled out: to be happy, be nice, and just keep trekking. In a nutshell, this pretty much sums up the dispute of every argument I ever had with him.

I didn't realize the power of my dad's wisdom until after he died. His purpose on Earth was to make me a better person. Yes, my dad left too soon and I would give anything for him to be here with me right now, but when he died, he left a piece of himself here on this earth. That piece is Kathryn and me. We are direct reflections of the person he was.

But in many ways, it's the small things, the things that would once annoy me, that constantly remind me my dad isn't here anymore. It's not seeing him come home on a Tuesday night after playing golf. It's not getting a kiss goodnight from him and not getting told it's time for bed at 10 p.m. And it's the absence of those endless questions that he used to ask, those endless questions that would embarrass me and annoy me.

Those questions are truly what I miss the most. Every night on the way home from gymnastics he would "interrogate" me on my day, as I used to say. He would ask me how my day went, I would tell him something, and he would respond with a follow-up question. And another. And another.

So how much of my "daily outline" would he remember? My mom and I would attest to the fact that he probably didn't remember much. In the same way I remembered to do my homework yet would forget to fold a load of laundry, my dad only used to remember information that he wanted to remember. He used to remember the exact layout of every hole at every golf course where he had ever played, yet he couldn't remember the name of my friend's dad whom he saw every week.

If my mom had asked him when we got home what Sarah had done that day, there's a good chance he wouldn't remember much besides some small detail that he found exceptionally interesting. But that didn't matter. He was interested in my life. He wanted to know what was going on in gymnastics, even if he didn't understand any of the terminology. He wanted to know what classes I was taking and what subject material I was learning, whether he had learned it "back in the days" or had never heard of it at all.

And despite how annoying it was at the time, I lie in bed trying to fall asleep some nights and I can't get the sound of his voice out of my head. Most nights I talk to him and tell him about my day, and sometimes I hear him asking me questions and responding with his typical phrase, "Well, excellent!" when I tell him of an unusual accomplishment of mine. It may sound crazy to some people, but I honestly believe my dad is with me wherever I go. I wear red bracelets that I designed in support of ALS awareness, and all I have to do is look down at them to know he is with me.

I'll never forget the time at an important gymnastics meet when I truly felt his presence before I was about to begin my floor routine. It's hard to describe, but all of a sudden I was just overcome with a sense that he was there. My mom would later tell me that she had a strange feeling that Dad was with her when I was doing my routine. That is too ironic for him not to have actually been there with us, and it's no coincidence that he was with both of us just then. He knew I could do my routine well and I didn't need any help; I just needed to be reminded that he was watching. When I started, he went up into the stands with my mom to watch. I told him, a few weeks before he died, that I knew it would be difficult, but all I wanted was for him to come to just one gymnastics meet. And at this meet in Virginia Beach, Virginia, I believe he truly was there.

Call it religious or spiritual or crazy or whatever you want, but his presence at the meet was real. I needed my dad, and he was there. I know there will be countless more times in the future when my dad should have been with me and he will not: when I graduate from high school, get my first job, and get married. And it will hurt when he is not be there to kiss me goodbye or walk me down the aisle, when I want to call him on a Sunday night to talk to him about what I did that week, and when he will not get to witness the milestones in my life that he had planned on seeing. I'm not going to try to be all positive here, because the reality is that it hurts every day that I wake up and don't see his face. And it sucks not being able to watch Sunday Night Football with him. And no, it is not okay that he is not going to be here for me during all the times I need him.

But there is some comfort, however small it may be, that he is watching over us. I like to call him my very own guardian angel that is always with me. If I didn't believe this, if I didn't know this, then I don't know how I would be able to move forward, how I could live in this world without my father physically here. There is some small comfort in saying, "I love you" to him in Heaven every night, because that is the last thing I told him when he was here on Earth, and I know he is always listening. Maybe this is a way of reaching acceptance too.

Summer, 2012

The day after Dad was diagnosed with ALS. Still looking pretty healthy! This was the night Mom asked me if I wanted to go to Paris with Dad. June 17th, 2012.

Two months after diagnosis, Dad still wanted to take his signature jumping picture—even if he could only get a few inches off the ground. August, 2012. Skagway, Alaska

One of the greatest nights of my life, walking on the beach at night with the whole family — including the dogs. August, 2012.

And 704 steps later, Dad and I made it to the top of the Eiffel Tower. He barely broke a sweat. September, 2012. Paris, France.

That smile never stopped.

One of my favorite pictures of me and Dad. July, 2013

Just To Make You Smile ~ 186~ Sarah Caldwell

Dad with Finnegan, his only
male companion in the house!

Right after we went swimming in the ocean.
April, 2013. Cayman Islands.

The day I took Dad golfing for Fathers Day.
June 16th, 2013. Exactly one year after

Our Fight Against ALS

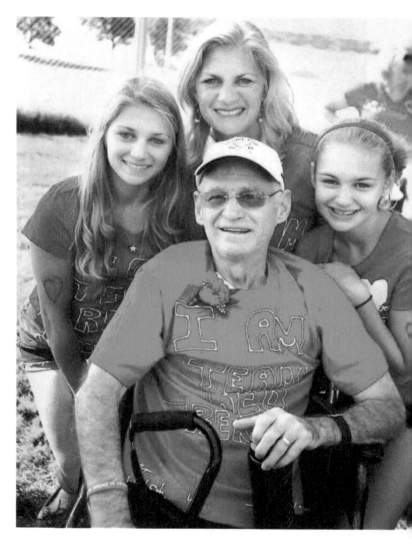

The Walk to Defeat ALS. September 7th, 2013.
One month before Dad died.

Just To Make You Smile ~ 190~ Sarah Caldwell

Crossing the finish line at the ALS Walk.

Kathryn, Mom, and me on Capitol Hill for the National
ALS Advocacy Conference in DC. May, 2014

Chapter Ten

I'll always remember the first time my parents talked to us about our guardians. They were going to Italy, and they told us if anything happened to them while they were there, we would go to live with my aunt and uncle. I knew nothing was going to happen to them and I would see them in ten days, but as a nine-year-old girl, I couldn't help but feel tears well up in my eyes at the thought of both my parents dying. It was such a distant thought and a seemingly impossible situation that I quickly brushed it off, forgetting about this conversation for years, but then my mom was diagnosed with cancer.

We were in New Jersey visiting family, and my mom and dad sat Kathryn and me down on the porch one afternoon. My mom told us she needed surgery to remove something that was in her stomach. I knew something was wrong, so I guess I wasn't all that surprised, and I certainly wasn't very worried. On the day of the surgery, Kathryn and I were at a friend's house, and when my dad called and I asked how it went, I didn't get the, "Just fine, she's doing great," answer I was expecting. He told us it went "okay." That's one word you never want to hear after someone has surgery. Okay means it hadn't gone as planned, that something unexpected had happened. Only later would I find out that the tumor they removed from her abdomen was larger than a football.

After the surgery, my aunt and uncle came up to Maine to visit and we later went back to New Jersey with them as my mom recovered. The night before we left, I knew something wasn't quite right because my parents were being too friendly. When I asked my mom if the doctors knew more about the tumor, she said we would talk about it later. "It's not cancer, right?" I asked. She didn't respond. Well, there was my answer.

That night at dinner my mom told us she had a very rare form of sarcoma cancer, but that she wouldn't need any more treatments unless it came back. I didn't ask too many questions, and although they told me not to Google this type of cancer because it was so rare, of course that was the first thing I did that night. There wasn't much information, and I honestly didn't dig too deep because my parents didn't even seem too concerned. Overall, it didn't seem like it was cancer; after all, with no chemotherapy or radiation and no more surgeries, how bad could it really be? The answer: really bad. They didn't tell me that there are only hundreds of people every year that are diagnosed with this kind of cancer. They didn't tell me that it was almost guaranteed that the cancer would come back and my mom would need more treatment. They didn't tell me that she wasn't expected to be here in a few years.

So flash forward to June, 2012, when my dad was diagnosed with ALS, and, by some kind of miracle, my mom was in remission after an immediate reoccurrence, radiation, and another surgery. By October of 2013, the month my dad died, she was still in remission, almost three years cancer-free. There is no reason why she is still alive today other than the fact that God or whoever else is in charge saw that her girls needed a mother to raise them. A diagnosis of ALS has no hope for remission; there was no hope for my dad to get better. But my mom did get better, and that is the single most thing I am grateful for in life. But that's not to say her cancer won't come back. Every six months when she goes in for her CAT scan, my hands stay glued to my phone, waiting for the text from her saying that the scan is clean, waiting for that moment where I can finally breathe normally again, because I have another six months before I have to worry again.

But having just one parent left, my heart skips a beat even more than just that moment when I see that twice a year text; my heart skips a beat every time I'm at school or gymnastics or anywhere else and I am informed someone needs to talk to me or I have a message waiting for me in the office.

All it takes is a crazy driver who blows a red light, a single piece of plaque that builds up in an artery and causes a massive heart attack, and I could become an orphan. If I think the sound of being raised by a "single mother" sounds awful, well, just the sound of the word "orphan" is a hundred times worse. It makes me think of the abandoned children in Russia or China or some other country, the children who line up, praying that a family will bring them back to their home. It makes me think of kids whose parents are drug addicts and alcoholics and who are subsequently bounced from foster home to foster home. It makes me think of what my sister and I would become if my mom died.

So on that day in February when the phone rang in math class and my teacher said I needed to go to the office, of course the first thing I thought was that something had happened to my mom. I knew I hadn't gotten in trouble (or at least, I didn't think I had), and I couldn't think of any other reason why I would have been called down *right now*. I picked up my textbook and coffee cup and walked very slowly to the office. I didn't want to know who was behind those doors, who was there to tell me something I didn't want to hear.

As I walked in, the cheerful attendance secretary told me to go into the conference room. I slowly peered through the door and saw the principal, vice principal, superintendent, Holly, my mom, and her friend Jan, who was visiting from out of town. I don't really remember what anyone said to me, but I just remember seeing the look on my mom's face and seeing her smile through the tears of joy.

Mr. Palmer, the principal, held up an official looking document and told me I had been selected as the High School Honoree for the Prudential Spirit of Community Awards. My jaw literally dropped and I just stared at him. This award was something Holly had encouraged me to apply for back in November, so at the last minute I wrote an essay describing my work for ALS advocacy and fundraising and how I had helped make a positive impact on the community. Not to sound stuck up, but when I read the biographies of previous honorees, I thought I might have had a good shot at earning some type of recognition, but the thought of being named an honoree for the state of Maine didn't enter into my mind a whole lot because of what it entailed: an all expenses paid trip to Washington DC where I would join an honoree from each one of the fifty states for a series recognition events.

All the adrenaline was causing my heart to race at high speed, but I couldn't manage to say anything other than "thank you" as people were congratulating me. In fact, other than the initial jaw drop, I don't think I showed much emotion at all. I knew this award was a huge deal. I knew I would be going to DC to meet with other kids whose stories were equally or more amazing than mine. It was so incredible it seemed as if it couldn't possibly have been happening. My mom had tears in her eyes and Jan was trying to take a bunch of pictures while everyone was shaking my hand. My mom came over and gave me a hug. I felt her tears against my cheek. She was so proud of me.

The only problem was, the person whose congratulatory hug I wanted the most, the person who had inspired me to do everything that earned me this award, wasn't there. The person in each state receiving this news that day was probably jumping up and down with excitement, but the person from Maine was speechless, overwhelmed, and about to start crying because the only reason she was receiving this award was because her dad got sick.

If my dad hadn't been diagnosed with ALS, I wouldn't have started all these fundraising and advocacy campaigns. Instead of being in a room with some of the most important people in the school district, I would have been in advisory with Ms. Magnuson, probably listening to one of her life lessons like "Don't marry for looks" or "Don't eat Splenda, it will kill you," as I drink my coffee full of Splenda. Besides, I felt so awkward accepting the award when everything that I had done was for the pure benefit of others; it was all things I had chosen to do because I wanted to help others with ALS. I didn't want anyone to think I had done all of it to win some award.

After a few more minutes of chatter and more pictures, I gave my mom one last hug and headed out into the swarm of people bustling through the hallway. I felt like a different person. I went to advisory where I told Ms. Magnuson the news, still not sure whether I should have been happy or sad or a mixture of both. She was of course, excited for me, but she also understood my feelings of uneasiness. At the same time, she told me I deserved this award. She told me the money I raised would help so many people with ALS and that my effort should be recognized. And as Holly told me, which is why I applied to for this award in the first place, the award had the potential to draw so much attention to ALS. It would put this disease out in the local media again, and there would be even more opportunity for fundraising.

As soon as I got home from school before heading off to gymnastics, I saw the giant package on the counter containing all the "official" forms from Prudential. It was an even bigger deal that I had thought…if that is even possible. Jan walked in the room and asked if my mom had told me the news. I had no idea what she was talking about, no idea what would be making her so excited as she was talking to me.

Well, something that I could never have imagined. I would be in DC for four days as part of the Prudential Award, and as mom subsequently informed me, the National ALS Advocacy Conference, the conference that I had read so much about and wanted to attend so badly, started the day after the Prudential events were over. Now, I am not the kind of person who believes that everything has to happen for a reason, but in that instant, I knew it had to be more than a coincidence. I knew there had to be a purpose to my receiving the award beyond simply getting all the recognition. Little did I know this purpose would stem much deeper than I ever would have thought.

* * * * *

The next few months were full of even more firsts in this new life without my dad: the first Valentine's Day where there were no roses and flowers laid out on the counter from him; the first time I won Vault at a gymnastics competition and didn't go home to a hug from my dad, or better yet, a perplexed question of, "You stuck it, why didn't you get a perfect 10?!" (Sorry, Dad, it doesn't work like that); and the first time my mom spent their wedding anniversary twirling her rings on her finger, receiving flowers and cards from Kathryn and me rather than her soul mate.

It was the first time I was interviewed for a newspaper article and had to talk about my dad in the past tense rather than the present. I remember this first time very clearly. Just a few weeks after I found out I had won the award, my mom, Emma, and I were in Virginia for a gymnastics meet. The day after we competed, where I won that first Vault title of the year, we were at lunch when I got a phone call from a reporter who wanted to interview me about the award.

I brought my iced tea outside the restaurant where I sat on a wooden bench and began talking to this man. He asked me basic questions from what my dad did for work ("helping businesses save money," his favorite thing to do in life) to how much money I had raised for ALS research ("$23,000 and that number is still growing," to which I received a response of, "wow, that's a lot") to what this award is called ("The Prudential Spirit of Community Awards, sponsored by the National Association of Secondary School Principals"). Then he got to the hard parts: he wanted me to tell him about what it was like finding out my dad had ALS. And so, I went on a rant about how I found out my father was going to die by finding a bottle of medication, telling my story all the way up until the day he died and how I felt as though I was to blame because I got him sick. I didn't realize how much I had been rambling on until after I finished my last sentence and looked at the clock on the building across the street. I had been talking for fifteen minutes straight, raw emotion intertwined with every fact.

I felt terrible for putting all of that on him. I hadn't meant to spill to him all the raw emotions; I was just planning on talking about the award and my work for ALS. "It's okay," he said. "You've been through a lot. Thank you for sharing it with me." Those words touched me in some way. I had shared my story with someone for the first time.

For the first time, I had chronicled my decision of making something positive out of my dad's devastating diagnosis because I knew it had the potential to help others.

The next day the article appeared online and then in the local newspaper. By the time I got back to Maine, I had received countless emails and texts from people congratulating me on the award, and whereas the week before I might have had feelings of uneasiness, this time I was full of gratitude for everyone's support and for my opportunity to receive this award. That interview changed me; I realized the award truly did have the potential to further my cause. That interview was followed by another interview (which, thankfully, went much more smoothly) and another lovely article that was published in another newspaper.

Over the next few months the hype of everything died down (thank goodness), but it picked right back up again towards the end of April as the May 1st departure date for D.C. got closer and closer. First of all, let me say that in going to this thing, I had to a.) miss my junior prom, and b.) miss gymnastics Eastern Nationals (which, as it turned out, I wouldn't have been able to go to anyways because I injured my foot in the middle of my floor routine at Regionals — just another thing that complicated my life). In any event, right before I left for D.C., Holly and Mr. Palmer, the principal, organized an assembly that hundreds of people from the school attended to recognize me for my award, once again stirring up the "excitement" about this whole thing.

To tell you the truth, I was less than thrilled about the idea of getting on stage in front of all these people and accepting a medallion from a Prudential representative. But then I thought about the sole reason I had applied for the award in the first place: to continue to spread awareness of ALS. Yes, most people in the school knew about ALS because of my family, but did they really know what it was all about? I could make them sit there and watch me get presented with a medal and wonder if they thought I did all of this for the fame and recognition, or I could give the assembly a higher purpose.

So, with the seats in the auditorium full and my mom, Kathryn, the Prudential representative, and a woman from the ALS Association sitting right next to me, a video flashed across the screen on the stage. Prudential gave the honorees the option of making a "promotional" video describing our work, and I hadn't planned on making one simply because I didn't have the time, but the weekend before, I was blessed (yes, blessed, because it never happens) with the occurrence of having no homework, so I dedicated a Sunday to making the video. I set up a camera and awkwardly talked to a wall all afternoon as I "interviewed" myself, but I got my message across. This was the video all the people in auditorium were watching as I stared into their eyes trying to decipher their looks. I sat up there uneasily, looking down at the big clunky cast on my leg and wishing that I wasn't up there at that moment.

In the video I talked about my dad being diagnosed with ALS and his frustration, not over the fact that he got sick — people get sick, after all — but over the fact that there was no effective treatment or cure for ALS, no hope for him ever to have gotten better. I talked about my agonized frustration as I watched him struggle to do basic tasks such as tying his shoes, brushing his teeth, and eating breakfast. Then I moved forward into discussing the fundraising and advocacy I had done, ultimately inspired by my dad's message to all of us in life of being kind, happy, and trekking along. Pictures flashed across the screen from the Walk and then moved to dozens of people wearing their red bracelets in support of ALS and my dad. I ended the video with my main message to everyone: none of this work will bring my dad back, but it will directly impact those in the future afflicted by this awful disease. Yes, it was the thing I had done to prevent myself from being sad, but in the end, I suppose if I had to do something, it was the best thing I could have done, because it made a positive impact on the lives of others.

Mr. Palmer then got up to say a few works, followed by the woman from the ALS Association and the guy from Prudential whose name I never got. I honestly had no idea what they said, but I think it was along the lines of, "Sarah is an incredible person and is so selfless and incredible and finds the silver lining in everything, including her broken foot." (the words of Mr. Palmer, always lightening the mood).

When it came time for me to "say a few words," I hopped up on one foot to the microphone, my boot dangling to the side. My mom had told me to be prepared to say something, but I brushed it off because already knew what I was going to say (which, in my terms, meant I was going to wing it). Well, when I actually got up there, I suddenly didn't know where to begin. There was no way to fully express what I was feeling and what I wanted to say, so I'm sure whatever I said made me sound frazzled, but what I hope I got at is that the award was very much an award for the students of Falmouth High School and my family as much as it was mine. My friends, the faculty, and people I didn't even know were the ones who had showed up at the ALS Walk, who bought bracelets and still wore them to this day, who wore red and made me giant cards when my dad died, and who had supported me through a very difficult year, lending a smile or a hug when I seemed to need it most; my family, my mom, Kathryn, and all the relatives who have always "showed up," were the ones who had been by my side every step of the way, who had the same passion and drive to find a cure for ALS as I did, and who loved me unconditionally no matter how hyped up I got.

And so, as I told all the people in the auditorium, we *will* find a cure for ALS. This cure may not have been found in time to save my dad, and it may not even be able to save people in the next year — it may be a lifetime from now — but we will find it. ALS is an insidious disease that has a death rate of *one hundred percent*, a number that needs to be changed, and this can only be done if more attention is drawn to this disease and more funding is subsequently allocated to research for a cure. Maybe I couldn't save my dad, but, with their help, I told them, I am confident we will be able to save the fathers and mothers and friends and coworkers of the future.

* * * * *

In any group of people, there is bound to be that one person everyone secretly hates because he or she is rude, mean, obnoxious, or just plain weird. Among the group of one hundred two kids selected by Prudential for this award — one middle school student and one high school student from every state plus D.C. — I can honestly say not one person fit that description. I met Elijah, who organizes events to put smiles on the faces of foster children, Ellie, who collects golf clubs for inner city kids to get them off the streets, Kinsey, who raises hundreds of thousands of dollars for cancer and is a motivational speaker, Molly, who runs an adoption agency for abandoned turtles, Jessica, who builds safe houses for victims of sex trafficking in third world countries, and Sean who provides goods and services to veterans in military hospitals, among others, all who remind us of the good in the world, that there truly are selfless people out there who devote themselves to making a difference in the lives of others.

Together, we had formal dinners, toured national monuments, and shared our stories, stories that made each other cry and laugh. In four days, one hundred-two strangers came together and became a family. We joked that if we could all just be put in the same high school, it would be the greatest high school ever established, its potential to change the world limitless.

Sadly, the time came when we had to part ways to go back to each of our respective states, each of us thinking we would never see each other again. But social media has this thing about it, this thing that makes us as if we never parted. To this day, we all still communicate on Facebook, supporting one another in any way we can in our quests to change the world. I think that's what made this group of people so special—we have all changed the world in one way or another. Everyone had a story; everyone was special; everyone was there for a reason. Yes, my reason may have stemmed from the fact that my dad died, but the difference was in what I chose to do as a result. Every person there had a reason for doing what they did—Elijah had been an abused foster child; Kinsey had cancer as a child; Sean's father was a firefighter who died in 9/11, just to name a few.

The first night there, as we were all sitting in a ballroom, trying to remember the official table manners we had been taught an hour before, Barbara Jane ("BJ") Powers, the "principal of all principals" as I called her, told us to remember three things in life: show up, pay attention, and make a contribution. Showing up and paying attention, she told us, are the easy parts; making a contribution takes effort and distinguishes you from others. Finding your place in the world or a cause that inspires you may be challenging, but once you find it, boy is the challenge worth the result. Every single one of us in that room had made a contribution to this world in some way or another, but I can guarantee you that not one of us stopped once the Prudential event was over. In fact, we were all inspired to make our initiatives that much more meaningful.

For me, my next step began in the next few days when we attended the National ALS Conference.

* * * * *

As soon as I walked into the hotel where the conference was taking place, I saw a man in a wheelchair sitting in a corner, his wife beside him. My mom was checking in and I had nothing else to do, so I went over to say hi. The man wanted to know my connection to ALS, and I told him and his wife my dad had passed away from ALS several months ago and that I was able to be at this conference because I had won an award that allowed me go to D.C. that week. This man, whom I had never met before, started tearing up as I was telling him all of this. He was from Louisiana and had been diagnosed twelve years ago. He was confined to a wheelchair, but his diaphragm was amazingly at ninety-seven percent functional capacity. He told me it was people like me, people who were fighting this disease even after they had lost a loved one, that gave him hope for a cure. I will never forget the look on his face, the look of desperation, almost as if he was saying, "I have held on for this long, there has to be some sort of cure just around the corner." I never saw this man again at the conference.

I went to find my mom and Kathryn and we headed to the elevator. While waiting in line I saw a man I felt like I had seen before, but I couldn't quite place him. He was standing with a woman, and as the doors opened, we all walked into the elevator. I struck up a conversation with him about the conference in general, and then it hit me. This man's name was Anthony. ALS runs in his family. His grandmother had died of ALS, his mom was currently battling it, and he himself had just recently been diagnosed at age twenty-six. A local news station did a short documentary on him, and I somehow had come across it only days before.

"You're Anthony, aren't you?" I suddenly piped up. He seemed surprised that a strange young girl knew his name, but then I told him how I saw his video. I told him he was incredible. We talked for a few moments before he got off the elevator with his fiancée, Laarne.

Later that day I saw the two of them sitting on a couch in the lobby and I went to sit by them. He asked what was in the bag I was holding, and I pulled out all the gifts a group of people had given to all kids attending the conference: an iTunes gift card, a stuffed flamingo, a photo-frame travel coffee cup, a book about ALS, and so many other things that had brought tears to my eyes when I had first gone through the bag's contents. It's these small gestures from people I don't even know that continue to make my heart feel all warm and fuzzy; I had dedicated so much time to helping other people with ALS, and being on the other side of it all was incredible.

Anthony, Laarne, and I began to talk about the genetics of ALS (it is a running wonder of mine whether or not my dad's was genetic, as he has no other risk factors such as military service or repeated head trauma, but Anthony told me it probably isn't given the fact that we have no family history of any neurological diseases whatsoever). He told me about what he has been through with his mom and grandmother, and what his views on living with ALS were. I looked at this man and saw someone who had the option of falling into a hole of sorrow and depression upon receiving this diagnosis at such a young age, but as I have noticed about ALS patients time in and time out, he had an incredible view on life. He, like my dad, had chosen to live with ALS.

Over the next few days I met many more wonderful people. Carolyn, who had been diagnosed with ALS a few years before, became my "adopted grandmother" and new best friend at the conference. Karen, who, confined to a wheelchair and unable to speak, travels throughout her state of Oklahoma helping *other* people with ALS, gave me a blue bracelet to wear. And a man whose name I never got and who flew in all the way from Hawaii all while navigating the airports in his high speed power wheelchair gave me more inspiration to fight this disease. I looked into the eyes of these people and saw living proof of the fact that people out there need our help.

I used this inspirational drive as my mom, Kathryn, and I pled our case to our Maine congressmen on Capitol Hill about legislation that would benefit ALS. One particular initiative was gaining their votes to help fund the ALS Registry, which collects information on the demographics of ALS so that we can better understand who gets this disease. At the top of the list was also gaining their support for a petition against Medicare. Medicare had recently stopped funding any eye-tracking generating devices that have any form of "apps" on them — email, Facebook, you name it — because they are "unnecessary." Well, let me tell you something. My dad never made it to this point, but many people with ALS are confined to their homes, unable to speak and unable to move, their only form of communication through the movement of their eyes as tracked by this software. Denying them these devices — their only form of communication with the outside world — is denying them their basic rights. We had to convince the congressmen of this as well.

That day, we met with both senators from Maine, both of whom I had met only a few days before to receive congratulations on behalf of the Prudential award. We also met one representative and the other representative's aid. We told our story of our father having died of ALS, of the agony we went through seeing him struggle on a daily basis with no hopes of getting better. We pleaded them to support the initiatives to help make a difference in the lives of people living with ALS right now. And we gained the support of every person we talked to. On one of these meetings a man from the National ALS chapter sat in to listen, and he was so impressed with what we said that he bought us lunch after. Once again, the small things.

Upon returning to the conference that day, we attended lectures from scientists and doctors on the current research on treatments for ALS. Stem cells, cells that have the potential to turn into any kind of cell and to divide indefinitely, seem to be one of the most promising techniques in the search for a cure for ALS. My dad used to spend hours and hours researching stem cell clinical trials in hopes of prolonging his life by even a few months. Since research into using stem cells to treat ALS is still in the early stages, the only way to receive treatment is through a clinical trial.

Clinical trials are run through hospitals and private companies and enroll small populations of people to act as the guinea pigs for a new treatment. Since the results of patients will be used to analyze the effectiveness and safety of the treatment, there are tight restrictions put in place in order to minimize confounding variables that could skew the data and lead to inaccurate conclusions about the treatment. Clinical trials for ALS generally include people in the fairly early stages of progression, and my dad unfortunately progressed too quickly to be considered for any trial.

At the conference, we heard about the most up-to-date research on stem cells as well as the specific gene therapy methods that were being investigated for the genetic forms of ALS. After one of the scientists presented, there was a short period for questions. I shot my hand up in the air. My question had something to do with how a specific gene would be targeted and whether the goal was to remove the protein produced by the gene or simply to prevent the gene from working. I could tell from the look on her face that this woman was completely caught off guard by a question of this magnitude; she was probably expecting one of the typical general questions from someone asking why the technique wasn't in clinical trial stages yet or why it had taken so long to develop. To a question like that, she would have probably answered something along the lines of, "Science takes time and we're working as fast as we can." I don't even remember her answer to my question because I was too busy being distracted by the fact that all eight hundred heads in the audience had suddenly turned around to look at the person who had asked this question.

Of those eight hundred heads, the person whose attention I probably caught the most was a man named Steve. Steve's wife had recently passed away from ALS and I had talked to him briefly earlier in the day. After the research session was over he came up to me, amazed by the complexity of the question I asked. This man had equal or more energy and excitement about fundraising for ALS. We started talking about the exciting things in the field of ALS research, and he introduced me to a doctor who had spoken earlier named Merit Cudcowicz.

This woman wasn't the typical cold-hearted doctor and researcher; she was a genuine and kind and wonderful human being. As Steve told me, she'd made a special effort to fit his wife in to her clinic and would spend hours talking and emailing them about ALS and treatment opportunities. Her work involves a list of current clinical trials for ALS patients that aims at developing "novel treatments" for this disease. She is the one who has given me hope and reassurance that there will be a cure for ALS in the near future. After leaving the conference, I emailed her, thanking her for speaking at the conference and for taking the time to talk to me as well. Her response was one of the most thoughtful and elegant things I have ever read in my life. Coming from a doctor who probably had hundred things she could have been doing other than emailing a seventeen-year-old girl, that was pretty great.

After getting back from DC, life seemed to calm down a bit for me. I fell into a routine with the last few weeks of school and the beginning of an intense summer of gymnastics training. I was still distributing the awareness bracelets, but my ALS campaigning toned down for a few months.

But then there was this thing called the ALS Ice Bucket Challenge that swept the nation. It was started by a man named Pat Quinn and his friend, former Boston College baseball player Pete Frates. Both men had been diagnosed with ALS in their twenties. The premise behind the Ice Bucket Challenge was to film yourself dumping a bucket of ice water on your head and post the video to Facebook or another form of social media, challenging three other people to take part in the challenge to raise awareness of ALS. If you didn't want to douse yourself in ice water, you had to make a donation to the ALS Association or some other ALS organization.

I remember coming across something on Facebook about some "challenge" for ALS, but it wasn't until a friend who goes to Boston College texted me and told me about what was going on that I realized the scale of this whole thing. I was soon challenged by several people and made a video and posted it to Facebook. Before I knew it, my family and I were being mentioned in dozens of videos, with countless tributes to my dad. It wasn't long before everyone from Lady Gaga to George Bush to Tom Brady were taking part and challenging others to do so too. No one could turn on the news or log onto their Facebook account without mention of the Ice Bucket Challenge, which turned into one of the largest social media campaigns for a disease to date.

At the same time, in the eyes of Pat and Pete, the premise behind this challenge wasn't to raise money — it was to raise awareness of ALS, exactly what I have always been pushing for. People didn't have to donate unless they refused to accept the challenge, but they did anyway. Within two months, the ALS Association had received $115 million in donations, a monumental figure compared to the $2.5 million that was donated in the same time frame from the year before. This whole thing was proof of the message in the ALS campaign that I had been pushing for: the more people who know about the disease, the more funds that will be allocated towards helping find a cure. Suddenly this disease was no longer known as just Lou Gehrig's Disease — it was a disease people realized could affect those they would least expect.

At an ALS research conference I attended a few months afterward, where I once again had the privilege of speaking with Dr. Cudkowicz, I met Pat and his wife Jen. Pat is yet another person who has chosen to live with ALS, becoming immersed in the ALS community and participating in the quest to help find a cure. He and his buddies started the Ice Bucket Challenge as a fun way to draw attention to the disease, but they never thought it would reach the magnitude that it did. He challenged his friend Pete, and once the B.C. community and professional athletes got involved, well, the rest was history.

The whole Ice Bucket Challenge thing reached a magnitude where people began to get annoyed at it and tried to find the flaws in it, such as complaining it was contributing to the drought in California or that the money raised through the ALS Association was going to employee salaries (which, from speaking with the CEO of the ALS Association myself, is completely false). Before the Ice Bucket Challenge, ALS didn't receive much attention due to the relatively limited number of people who are affected by it, but now, it would be a safe bet to assume most people in the U.S. have heard of it. So when it started becoming annoying and drawing ridiculous negative claims, that was a good thing. Because, as Pat said, "That's what we wanted. We caught peoples' attention."

So with the hype of the Ice Bucket Challenge, ALS's status as an unknown and forgotten about disease may have changed, but that doesn't change the fact that there is still no cure. Just because there was $115 million more in funding doesn't mean the money will be there in the future; it is important to keep the hype going. And with the ALS Walk taking place in September just as the Ice Bucket challenges were dying down, there could not have been a better time for Team Red Trekkers to walk and raise awareness (and money) for ALS.

Like the year before, our influx of red dominated the area, with a few hundred people showing up and raising thousands of dollars in support of my dad. Only this year, we weren't walking alongside my dad; we were walking in memory of him. All the excitement and positive energy distracted me from what the meaning of the day was truly about. I have said all along the Walk is a "happy event," an event that gives us an opportunity to recognize all the love and support in the community, not an event that simply gives us a chance to dwell on what ALS has done to our family. And while this is true, this year I was so concerned about getting as many people as possible to come to the Walk and to honor my dad that I forgot to honor him myself.

Of course I thought about him every minute that I was helping organize everything and walking in the event (I seem think about him every minute of every day anyway), I didn't allow myself to get overly emotional. I had been on two morning shows the week before and was interviewed at the Walk as well, and once I am put in front of a camera, I immediately go on autopilot. Yes, that's denial, I know, and yes, I know if I don't let myself feel my feelings it's not good, but sometimes it's all I can do to stay sane. If I had stopped to think about where we were last year, how we thought we had at least a few months left with my dad instead of a few weeks, then there's no way I would've made it through even being at the Walk without breaking down in tears every few minutes. There's no way I would've been able to look at the pictures that we brought without being overwhelmed by a consuming sadness, the exact feeling I experienced when I got home and the adrenaline wore off.

Are there days when I feel like this consuming sadness defines who I am? Absolutely. Some days I just don't want to get out of bed and some days I miss my dad so much I want to spend hours in the shower so I can cry without anyone hearing me. So I guess it may seem strange when I say that, in some ways, I am actually happier now than I was last year at this time. In some ways, I am even happier than three years ago at this time when there was no indication my dad was even sick. I've realized life is a constant battle of ups and downs. There are some very low lows, and there are some very high highs. What makes these highs so special is that I have learned that in a mere instant, your life can change forever. All it takes is finding a bottle of medication, being called out of gymnastics practice, for your world to come crashing down.

I have learned to search out the small things in life that make me happy, the small things that "fill my bucket." I have learned getting a B on a test is not the worst thing that could happen to me on a given day because I don't know what the rest of the day will bring. I have learned that happy moments, the moments you would want pictures of to fill a scrapbook, are the ones that need to be ingrained in the scrapbook in your mind. We have the tendency to remember only the bad things during the day, the people who honk their horns at us in traffic or are rude to us in the Starbucks line; instead, I try to pick out the small things that make me happy: a good song playing on the radio, a nice conversation with my mom, a woman at the grocery store who gives me an extra warm smile.

If you've noticed, I use the word *try* a lot in this book. I really like this word. The Oxford Dictionary says when you try to do something you "make an attempt or effort to do something." Some dictionaries say it is making an attempt while others say it is making an effort, but Oxford includes both. For argument's sake, let's pretend the definition says you have to both make an attempt *and* an effort in order for it to be classified as a "try."

Yes, I make an attempt to appreciate things in life that are easy to take for granted, but until I actually make an *effort*, I am not truly trying. Every day I say I try to remember to empty the dishwasher, but does brushing my mom off when she reminds me, insisting I will do it "later," constitute trying? Well, according to my previous statement, that response would be a negative. Okay, I'll work on it — I will make an *effort* to remember next time (you're welcome, Mom!)

At the same time, nowhere in the definition does it say that you have to be successful in what you are doing; all it says is that you have to make an attempt. Every day I try to remain optimistic about what the day will bring, but not all days am I successful. Some days I just feel plain sad. And that is okay. As I've stressed, it is okay not to be okay.

My dad was supposed to see me graduate from high school. I always dreamed of the day he would walk me down the aisle when I got married and the tears that would flood his eyes. He was supposed to get old and grumpy and forget who I was before he died. But none of that would ever happen. This was not what was supposed to happen. My parents did not get married and plan on one of them dying while their children were still growing up. My mom could not ever have imagined being left to raise two daughters on her own. As their friends used to say when they were in the peak of their "social years," they all planned on growing old together and living in some retirement home with a wide front porch and my dad there in his white overalls being the handyman who had to stay busy and help anyone by fixing the drain in their little apartment or something. Out of all the people in this group of friends, no one expected my dad to go first. He was always the healthiest, the one in the best shape, the one who took care of himself the most (let's forget about the time he decided to jump through that fire, subsequently tripping and falling straight in to the blazing hot coals…).

My parents planned to be there for each other until the ripe old age of a hundred, side by side through sickness and in health. My dad was there every step of the way for my mom's cancer battle. And my mom was certainly going to be there right alongside my dad for the fight of his life. But even after they found out it was ALS, my dad was supposed to have four to seven years to live, not just sixteen months. We were prepared to fight, but somehow things just didn't work out that way. I wasn't supposed to lose my dad, my superhero, at age sixteen. But somehow I did. No child is supposed to lose a parent. But somehow it happens every day to children all around the world.

I try to appreciate all the things I have in life, how much love people have for me, how lucky I am to have a warm bed to fall asleep in every night, because for every bad thing that has happened to me, there have been a hundred good things. Some days I am grateful, while other days I dwell on aspects that I feel make "life not fair." I used to tell that to my dad all the time whenever he made me empty the dishwasher or help him with yard work — "Life is not fair, Dad. My friends don't have to do all of this." And, as he would tell me every time, "I never said life was fair. It's just the way it is though." It is not fair that my dad died, but that is just the way it is.

One time I asked my mom if she and my dad would have done anything differently if they'd known he was going to get sick, whether they would've had kids sooner or taken an extra vacation. My mom laughed. If they had had kids earlier, they wouldn't have had Kathryn and me! And even if they had known my dad would get ALS, there's nothing they could have done to stop the disease from progressing. Besides, the life we have lived and the time we spent together as a family is something that none of us would change.

At the same time, there is exactly zero certainty as to what life will bring. We found out my dad had six months to live, but it turned into six weeks. It is cliché, I know, but the best thing I can say is live every day as if it were not only your last day, but your last day with the people you love because you do not know if you will receive a terminal diagnosis that day or get hit by a bus on the way to work. It's a hard thing to live by, I know, because so much stuff in life is always going on. In the end, it's not about going to see the world and going on that one last trip, because all that effort is simply not worth it. It's all about time. Would I have wanted to take another trip with my family when my dad was still here? No. I would have chosen to be more present. And that's what I'm trying to do now. It's all about how I can touch others in my life, because if it's true that we are "all here as God's instruments on Earth" as my mom says, it's about finding ways to make a difference in the lives of people you know and the lives of people you don't know. And that means being present.

As my mom says, in those last six weeks with my dad, when there were dishes in the sink and bills that needed to be paid, she thought that's what needed to be done. But even to this day, she says she wishes she had been even more in the moment, because although she would often put everything aside just to spend time with him, it never seemed like it was enough. None of us knew we had six weeks left with him, but all that summer, we worked on being present. It wasn't important to do the laundry; it was important to sit down and take the time to simply be with this man, this father, this husband, who was the light of our life, who taught us that the most important things in life are just to be happy, be nice, and keep on trekking.

Epilogue

I wish that I could say it gets easier. I wish I could say that, one year later, it doesn't hurt as much when I think of the fact that I don't have a dad anymore. Today is October 2nd, 2014. It is exactly one year since Dad died.

On this brisk fall day, as I sit by his grave writing this and eating a red lollipop that a sweet old man just gave me, I can feel myself clinging to all memories I have of him — the sound of his voice, the warmth of his hugs, the aggravated feeling I would get whenever he asked me a stupid question that he already knew the answer to but would ask anyway just to fill the space in a conversation. One year ago I woke up on an ordinary day, got ready for school, and kissed him goodbye, saying, "I love you."

I have not felt the warmth of my dad's hands in exactly one year. I have not given him a hug or had a conversation with him or said, "I love you" to him in exactly one year. One year later, I would give anything for him to ask me a stupid question, because I would happily answer it. I would fill my answer with paragraphs and paragraphs of useless details, if I could just talk to him one more time.

It doesn't get any easier. It gets harder. And as I sit here, staring at his headstone, a lawnmower buzzing in the background, the tears are streaming and they don't seem to want to stop.

Today marks the end of a year of firsts without my dad — the first Thanksgiving, Christmas, Father's Day, wedding anniversary, birthday, and so many more. Today marks the first day this cycle will begin again, because today is the second first day that I am living in this world without my father.

My mom made me go to church this morning, and for those of you who know me, church is not always the thing that's on the top of my list of priorities. But I went today because, in addition to making my mom happy, I figured it was a place where I could talk to my dad. As I was sitting there, daydreaming, I heard the priest say, "guardian angel." Indeed, today is the Feast of the Guardian Angel, whatever that means. So I decided to listen, and for the first time, I really got something out of going to church. He said today is the day we recognize the guardian angels who are sitting there on our shoulders. Message to you, Dad: good job dying on October 2nd, because I can't think of any day more appropriate than today to be called into Heaven to become my guardian angel.

A few months ago I came across a poem that made me tear up a bit. Now, on this one year anniversary, it makes the tears flow more than ever.

God saw you getting tired
And a cure was not to be
So he put his arms around you
And whispered
"Come to Me"

With tearful eyes we watched you
And saw you pass away
And although we love you dearly
We could not make you stay.

A Golden heart stopped beating
Hard working hands at rest
God broke our hearts to prove us
He only takes the best

It's right. God only takes the best. My dad's suffering is over — it's been over for an entire year now — but that doesn't change the fact that I would have devoted my entire life to making his suffering more bearable.

This year has been full of many incredible things, things that I am so grateful to have been a part of, but many of these things happened because my dad got sick. If he hadn't gotten sick, I would have never started a team for the ALS Walk. I never would have become close with Holly and her daughter, Louisa, and in turn, I would have never started coaching little kids in soccer, the joys of my Friday afternoons in the fall. I never would have gone to Mississippi to build a house for a family whose house was destroyed by Hurricane Katrina in 2005 and buried a Red Trekkers bracelet in the foundation. I never would have found a calling to helping others in any way I can. I never would have applied and won the Prudential Award and I never would have met the incredible people there. I never would have gone to the National ALS Conference, and I never would have heard the stories of these people. I never would have been able to help put on a benefit concert through the Service Club at the high school in support of ALS. I would have never been on live TV on many occasions during the frenzy of the Ice Bucket Challenge or attended the ALS conference in Florida. I never would have been labeled a leader in my school. I never would have been called out yesterday for "turning a terrible situation into something good through one selfless act after another" by an author and inspirational speaker who came to the school and whom I had never even met before (needless to say, I was MIA at the assembly in which he called me up, as I took the time to chill with Ms. Magnuson and some other friends to try to calm my rollercoaster of emotions on the eve of "the day").

If my dad hadn't gotten sick, I would not be the person I am today. It has been a year defined by extreme highs and extreme lows. These highs were some of the greatest moments of my life, but at the same time, I would give them all up if it meant my dad were still with us today.

What if someone told you everything happens for a reason, that even the bad things in life—every bad grade, every injury, every death—had a purpose? Well, if someone ever told me that, I like to say I would punch them in the face, but in reality I probably would just come up with an incredibly sassy comeback, listing all the reasons why, in fact, everything does *not* happen for a reason.

If anyone can come up with a reason as to why, at age sixteen, I was left without my superhero and best friend and thrown face first into the Dead Dad Club, and why, at age seventeen, I am still searching for reasons as to why my dad was so unfairly taken from me, I would like to know, because I have tried and tried to find a reason and I sure can't figure it out. As I am sitting here today, I can't help but look at his headstone—his shiny, polished headstone that actually has the wrong date of birth printed on it—and feel angry that this has happened to me. If everything happened for a reason, then my dad's death would simply be "the plan" for me in life. It would be my fate to live a life defined by talking about my dad in the past tense rather than the present.

People talk about fate as what you are destined to become and experience and whom you will inevitably meet. But does this mean that a person's fate is certain and cannot be changed? I would argue that fate is what you *ultimately* become and experience and whom you *coincidentally* meet. So was it my dad's "fate" to be diagnosed with ALS and die sixteen months later, my fate to live in this world without my father? No. There is no "plan" for how we are going to live our lives because we are the ones who ultimately choose what to do with the cards we are dealt.

At the same time, no matter how bad the situation, your fate is what was meant to happen because it is what has shaped your life as it is today. If my dad hadn't been diagnosed with ALS, I would have never experienced all the things I have in the past year. I never would have learned the lesson that it only takes one moment for your life to be changed forever.

So does all of this mean my dad did in fact die for a reason? Maybe not. Maybe there was not a reason. Although I am certain I would not be the same person I am today, hold the same values, and cherish the same experiences and memories I do today, I can only imagine what life would be like if my dad hadn't gotten sick: the fourth seat in the car would be filled when we drive to go see a movie; his office would have stacks of papers in every corner, and he would be fixing and installing little things around the house every weekend rather than his friends doing it for us. This is what I imagine life would be like. Nonetheless, I don't have any business thinking about what "could have" happened and what my life could be today because this is the way things are. This is my fate as it is now, and I cannot change what has already happened.

Even if my dad were still alive, while walking across the street one day, he could be hit by a bus and die. He could fall victim to a deadly virus. He could have had some blockage in his heart or aneurysm in his brain that has been building up his entire life and he would have died anyway.

Either one of these situations could have been his fate, and my fate and subsequent life would be right around where it is today in the "Dead Dad Club." But fate is sometimes uncertain, and there is no way to know what tomorrow will bring.

We constantly face the "what ifs" in life, the "what ifs" that have the potential to alter the course of our lives, to determine our fate. Yes, our decisions influence our fate, but these decisions often mirror the chance events that we encounter. It's a common notion that bad things happen to good people, the fate of these good people suddenly turning from optimistic and lively to dark and uncertain upon the arrival of this "bad thing." After my dad died, my fate could have been falling into a hole of sadness and never coming out, but I chose to live life the way my dad would have wanted me to: I chose to remain optimistic and help others suffering from this dreadful disease. So when I say bad things happen to good people, it is true, and there is nothing anyone can do to change this. But just because something bad happened does not mean your fate is horrible. Maybe your fate is not certain and maybe these events have the potential to sway your life in a direction you don't want to go, but you certainly have the power to change your fate, to decide how you want to live life and choose what kind of mark you want to leave on this world.

I have chosen to leave my mark on the world — make my contribution to the world, as BJ would say — by helping others with ALS and those who are in my situation. A few months ago I was introduced to a girl, Karen, whose mom has ALS. She was having a hard time and needed someone to talk to. We texted back and forth and then finally worked out a time to have coffee. Seeing her for the first time, I looked at her face and saw where I was one year ago. I saw the fear as she described being worried about her mom every living minute of the day. With my dad, it was the fear that he would choke while taking a sip of water, the fear that his legs would crumple beneath him while he tried to stand up, the fear that he would stop breathing.

I looked into Karen's eyes and I saw this same fear. If God put me on this earth for a reason, well, maybe this is part of my reason. I began talking to her about everything, telling her the anger and sadness and annoyance and resentment I would feel whenever my dad coughed or choked. I told her how I felt like I had no one to talk to and how I felt so alone in this world. And whenever I said any of this, she would look right back at me and breathe a sigh of relief, relief that she was feeling the same exact thing. I became her person to text at three in the morning when she felt anxious or sad or depressed or angry or anything, with me doing the same thing in return. Because I get it, and I know she gets it, too. She is someone who has entered my life who never would have if my dad hadn't gotten sick, someone who has changed my life and someone whose life I have changed.

At the end of Junior year, one day I told Ms. Magnuson I was going to write a book. I had been thinking about it for a while, but this was the first time I actually vocalized it. As soon as I said it, I knew I had to make it happen. And all these months later, I find myself sitting here writing these final words-- and what better day to do so on the one year annivesary of his death?

So I'll leave you with one final thought, as in the words of my father. Be nice to others — making a difference in someone's life is as simple as giving someone seventy-five cents so they don't have to dig through their wallet searching for extra change to buy water, as someone did for me today. Be happy — because that's all one can ever do in life. And finally, life is messy and life sucks sometimes, but just know that you will get through it. So, as best exemplified by my dad, just keep trekking.

On this day, and every day, I live by these three things, and I encourage you to live by them too. I have lived by them, and I have become a better person. I have taken something terrible and turned it into something that has the power to change the lives of others. And, above all, as much as it hurts, as much as I still have not found a way to live in this world without my father, I know he is up there looking down over me, the guardian angel right by my side.

So Dad, I hope you're proud of me. Writing this book has, without a doubt, been one of the hardest things I have ever done, but it has also been one of the most rewarding. I have shared our story with the world, and as the sun peers out from the heavy clouds that have covered the sky the entire day up until now, in this instant I know you're there smiling down on me as I write these final sentences. I can see your radiant face watching over as you say, "You did good, Sarah." I can see that glowing smile of yours, that smile of pure love, knowing that I have and always will do everything I can just to make you smile.

Works Cited

Chapter Two:

Madsen, Amy. "Putting Labels on Types of ALS." MDA/ALS News Magazine. MDA: Fighting Muscle Disease, 1 Jan. 2012. Web. 17 Mar. 2014.

Kumar, David R. "Jean-Martin Charcot: The Father of Neurology." National Center for Biotechnology Information. U.S. National Library of Medicine, 30 Aug. 0005. Web. 17 Mar. 2014.

"Repairing and Replacing Damaged Cells." Neuralstem Cell Therapy. Neuralstem Inc., n.d. Web. 17 Mar. 2014.

"Amyotrophic Lateral Sclerosis." Muscular Dystrophy Association. N.p., n.d. Web. 17 Mar. 2014.

"Amyotrophic Lateral Sclerosis (ALS)-Topic Overview." WebMD. WebMD, n.d. Web. 16 Mar. 2014.

Chapter Three:

Axelrod, Julie. "The 5 Stages of Loss and Grief." Psych Central.com. N.p., 8 Nov. 2014. Web.

"The Five Stages of Grief - Grief.com - Because LOVE Never Dies."Griefcom Because LOVE Never Dies. N.p., n.d. Web. 01 Jan. 2015.

Chapter Nine:

Aronson, J. K. "Rare Diseases and Orphan Drugs." British Journal of Clinical Pharmacology. Blackwell Science Inc, n.d. Web. 31 Dec. 1969.

"Mental Breakdown." Wikipedia. Wikimedia Foundation, n.d. Web. 01 Jan. 2015.

Antao, Vinicius C., and D. Kevin Horton. "The National Amyotrophic Lateral Sclerosis (ALS) Registry." Journal Of Environmental Health 75.1 (2012): 28-30. Academic Search Complete. Web. 16 Apr. 2014.

"Congress Archives - The ALS Association Greater New York Chapter." *The ALS Association Greater New York Chapter.* N.p., n.d. Web. 13 May 2014.

"Estimates of Funding for Various Research, Condition, and Disease Categories (RCDC)." *US Department of Health and Human Services.* N.p., 7 Mar. 2014. Web.

"Funding Overview." *National Institute of Neurological Disorders and Stroke (NINDS).* N.p., n.d. Web. 13 May 2014.

"Incidence of ALS." *UC San Diego School of Medicine.* N.p., n.d. Web. 09 Apr. 2014.

Kasarskis, Edward. "The ALS Association." *The ALS Association.* N.p., n.d. Web. 13 May 2014.

"Latest Facts & Figures Report | Alzheimer's Association." *Latest Facts & Figures Report |*

Alzheimer's Association. N.p., n.d. Web. 13 May 2014.

Liewer, Steve. "Lou Gehrig's Disease Twice as Likely to Strike Military Veterans." *Omaha.com.*

N.p., n.d. Web. 13 May 2014.

"Military Veterans." - *The ALS Association.* N.p., n.d. Web. 13 May 2014.

"U.S. Breast Cancer Statistics." *Breastcancer.org.* N.p., n.d. Web. 12 May 2014.

Williams, James R. "Diagnosis Pathway for Patients with Amyotrophic Lateral Sclerosis:

Retrospective Analysis of the US Medicare Longitudinal Claims Database." *BMC*

Neurology. BioMed Central: The Open Access Publisher, 4 Nov. 2013. Web.

About the Author

Photo courtesy of Grace Fan

When she was fifteen years old, Sarah found out her father had the fatal disease ALS. Since then, Sarah has worked tirelessly towards her goals of raising awareness and funds for ALS research to honor her father and to try to help others who have this disease. In her dad's last months of life on earth, she began her campaign by inspiring over 250 community members to get involved in the Walk to Defeat ALS for Northern New England as part of "Team Red Trekkers." But that was only the beginning. Sarah has educated herself and others about the disease, developed a relationship with the staff of the ALS Association, and marketed several similar fundraising events throughout the area, inspiring and bringing the community together in a wonderful way. She continued all her work even after her dad passed away by creating a line of ALS awareness bracelets that she sold throughout the community and now distributes nationwide. It was no longer about just her dad; it was about helping others. Sarah made it her mission to carry on his legacy and to stay involved in a quest for a cure.

Sarah has received national recognition for her extraordinary advocacy and fundraising on behalf of the ALS Association. She traveled to Washington, DC in May 2014 to receive the Prudential Spirit of Community Award as Maine's top high school youth volunteer. She, her mom, and sister Kathryn also attended the National ALS Advocacy Conference where they were able to speak with doctors about current ALS research, meet with others affected by this disease, and speak with members of Congress about current legislation that supported ALS research. Six months later, Sarah was invited to another ALS conference where she was able to meet with ALS researchers and learn about ways to further her ALS advocacy campaign.

Sarah has spoken publicly, been interviewed by televisions news stations, and created a video about her work with ALS. She also connects with other people and families who are affected by ALS, sharing her story and offering support. She has done an extensive amount of research on ALS and current clinical trials, compiling information from doctors, scientists, and ALS specialists she has spoken with, in addition to research done on her own. Beyond the tricky scientific aspects of the disease, Sarah is also able to explain ALS in a way that everyone can understand, providing metaphors and analogies to support her discussion of the disease.

Sarah knows first hand how difficult it is to watch a parent succumb to a disease like ALS, but she takes life's most difficult challenges and tries to find positive ways to channel the pain into action toward helping others. She hopes she can inspire others to do the same.

She loves to hear from readers. You can reach her at sarah.caldwell@yale.edu.

Contributor: Holly MacEwan

Tell Us What You Think

We appreciate hearing reader opinions about our books. You can email us at Sedonia.guillone@gmail.com.

In Japanese "kokoro" means "heart," the deepest, best place of a human being. Kokoro Press titles are written from that place, to that place in you. Our heart to your heart.

www.kokoropress.com

CPSIA information can be obtained at www.ICGtesting.com
Printed in the USA
BVOW11s1640270515

401956BV00004B/4/P